DO THIS WITH YOUR MONEY

SIX STEPS TO LIVE YOUR DREAM LIFE & RETIRE RICH

DO THIS WITH YOUR MONEY

SIX STEPS TO LIVE YOUR DREAM LIFE & RETIRE RICH

NIKKI DUNN, CFP®

Published by Best Seller Publishing®, St. Augustine, FL
Best Seller Publishing® is a registered trademark.
Printed in the United States of America.

ISBN: 978-1962595063

For more information, please write:
Best Seller Publishing®
53 Marine Street
St. Augustine, FL 32084
or call 1 (626) 765-9750
Visit us online at: www.BestSellerPublishing.org

Contents

Introduction

My Money Story

Everyone has a money story that shapes how they handle their finances. Maybe your money story comes from something you watched your parents do or something you were taught growing up. Maybe watching what your spouse or best friend did with money shaped your habits today.

Or maybe your money story has to do with the fact that money was absolutely never talked about with anyone around you, and because of that, you don't really know how to "adult" with your money.

When I reflect back on what shaped my relationship with money, it's turbulent, yet quite poetic.

Money was the root of all problems as I was growing up. My mom had to put my brother's and my school clothes on layaway at Kmart every year. I remember wishing we could take them home, but she explained to us that she couldn't afford them yet. I vividly remember being embarrassed to get off the school bus because we got dropped off in the "poor kids" neighborhoods, while other kids got off at homes with two- and three-car garages.

My parents wanted to give us everything; they just actually couldn't afford to. Meanwhile, they went into massive amounts of debt.

As my mother would always say, they were robbing Peter to pay Paul all the time and constantly fighting about it with each other. They'd have to take out a payday loan here, float a check there, take something to the pawn shop, and hope it all worked out. It was no secret in the house that money was a big problem.

After years of staring with envy at the nice neighborhoods on the bus route, the best thing happened. My mom became a Realtor, and we were able to afford our first ever single family home (it had a two-car garage, and I got my own room for the first time—whoop whoop!). It was a big deal for us as a family. I still remember my brother and me beaming with pride getting off at the bus stop.

But why as a kid was I thinking the way I did? Why did I care what the other kids thought when they saw what bus stop I got off at? Why did I care that we had to put our school clothes on layaway? Well, kids are mean, and they'll be quick to tell you that you don't have the coolest new shoes or you live in a poor person's neighborhood. The other part, I think, was just my wild curiosity over why some kids have a lot and some don't.

Parents will go into debt to make sure their kids are happy and don't feel like they have "less than." Mine for sure did.

That new house didn't solve any of the underlying money problems, though. My mom still had to fight with my dad about irresponsible spending habits. My parents were still robbing from Peter to pay Paul. The debt still piled up. It all actually got worse. Ultimately, when I was 16, my brother and I watched our parents go completely bankrupt and divorce over money after 16 years of marriage. They were in debt that would take them a lifetime to get out of, after years of trying to make it work.

So, yeah, I learned what NOT to do with money at a young age.

I swore to myself as a teen, while watching my parents divorce, that I would be successful financially one day and I would never go through what my parents did. My experiences were fuel. I knew that feeling of shame getting off at the bus stop, then feeling prideful once we got our first house. I had felt both sides viscerally. I couldn't wait to graduate from high school and get to work in the real world and make the money that I thought would solve everything.

Coincidentally, in the same year we moved out of our home after the divorce, I met a boy named Chris. I just thought he was really cute when I saw him at the lunch tables, and I asked my friend to introduce us (go me for being so bold, come to think about it).

As fate had it, he was an ambitious 17-year-old himself, who wasn't as interested in school as he was getting out in the real world working. He worked for a mortgage company at the time and was able to get me a job there as a receptionist making $10 an hour. Now, in 2002 as a 16-year-old, that was a lot of money for me while other kids were making $5.75 an hour. Plus, my boss would throw us bonuses every year. I felt like I had hit the job jackpot.

While we were working at the mortgage company, Chris was reading the book *Rich Dad Poor Dad* by Robert Kiyosaki, which was about building wealth and achieving financial freedom. When I look back, it still to this day feels like an oddly magical coincidence, and poetic. As a girl who had just got done watching my parents go bankrupt and divorce over money problems, I was intrigued.

Chris bought Kiyosaki's CASHFLOW board game shortly after reading the *Rich Dad Poor Dad* book. It was a board game that taught about different professions and income, getting out of the "rat race" of living paycheck to paycheck, acquiring assets instead of liabilities, learning to grow your cash flow, and ultimately living off passive investing income. This was a board game we would take into work and play when I was answering phones on the weekends at the mortgage company. We would play often in our spare time—you know, just two normal teenagers (not).

At a very young age, I went from watching my parents go bankrupt to coincidentally, in the same year, learning via this CASHFLOW game that I would play with my new boyfriend about all of the actual mistakes my parents had made. I learned young not to take on too much debt. I learned how to live within my means and save my money. I am not one of those women who has a story of getting out of $50,000 of debt in a year. I never got to the point of taking on that kind of debt. I was strategic with school loans and credit cards. I knew debt was bad, not only from watching my parents, but also from my new CASHFLOW board game education.

My Definition of Success

I knew entrepreneurship was a pathway, but my definition of success had always been to climb a corporate ladder. I wanted to have a cushy salary and benefits, walk around in a suit, have my own office, and be a high-level executive. It just appealed to me, and I thought it would make me feel important. I am confident that if I hadn't changed my path, this is what I absolutely would have done.

I ended up hating corporate America, though. I would come home crying from my frustration at being micromanaged and not really feeling as important as I had hoped I would. I was not fulfilled, and I knew I wasn't living up to my full potential. Chris, who was about to be my fiancé, had watched me mope and cry my way to work every day.

He had begun a new business by this time and, seeing my misery, came up with the idea for me to help him out. So, after freaking out over the idea of losing the health insurance and 401(k) that came with my current job—and after a few bottles of wine—I finally said screw it and quit my job. I was ready to learn everything about running a business and being an entrepreneur.

Chris was a futures trader in the stock market at the time, which means he would try to buy and sell financial contracts to make a profit. Think about it like buying a piece of jewelry in the morning for $100 and then selling it by the end of the day to someone else for $150. Your profit is $50 for making the transaction happen. Trading in the financial markets is similar, and it sounded glamorous and appealing to me. I wanted to learn how to do it, but there were not many women traders back then, and I felt out of place.

I did it anyway. I soon had my hands full with a multitude of projects.

While I was helping Chris run the business operations and the financials, I learned how to trade futures myself. I learned how to also trade individual stocks and, in turn, as we built more wealth for ourselves, I learned how to actually manage money. I was dealing with numbers I never thought I'd ever see in my life.

I worked with accountants, investment advisors, and attorneys along the way, and I learned everything that I could about how wealthy people manage their money. I wanted to be an expert in finance and money management. After all, this was my lifelong obsession, figuring out how the rich get rich and stay rich.

Why Should You Listen to Me?

So, why am I writing this book, and why should you listen to me?

The process of money management is among the most important topics to understand, though it's the least taught and talked about subject in most of our lives. No wonder so many people feel that they can't get a grip on their financial situations.

As I was learning my new money management skills, I would ask my friends if they knew about things like high-yield savings accounts, or optimizing retirement accounts to reach multiple goals, and it was always a deer in headlights situation. They either didn't know, were embarrassed, or didn't care to talk about money. Maybe because it stressed them out or they felt it was taboo to discuss it.

I was just a finance nerd who loved talking about money. Why did no one want to talk about money with me besides men? Chris and his buddies talked about it all of the time!

She Talks Finance

This is why I eventually started an online community geared toward women (and everyone is welcome) to help them learn more about money and investing through She Talks Finance, and this is why I am writing this book. I want to tell the stories of the failures and successes I and others have had with money. I want to give you a framework to build a better financial future for yourself. I'll share my money philosophies and what I do with my own money.

Why should you trust me?

Well, fast-forward to today:

I am a CERTIFIED FINANCIAL PLANNER™ professional who has been trained in every aspect of financial planning, including cash flow management, investing, tax strategy, estate planning, and everything in between.

- I'm an active stock market investor of my own portfolio and have been for the past decade.
- I'm an expert in behavioral finance and keeping people on track mentally.
- I teach personal finance through my She Talks Finance online community.
- I mentor do-it-yourself investors on how to be a better investor and achieve a more holistically healthy financial life.
- I've run multiple seven-figure businesses with my husband. I have handled the finances for all of them, and I have experience in marketing, managing business operations, optimizing taxes for business owners, and more.

It's Expensive to Get Help

I realized something pretty important in the finance world. It's really expensive to get help from a professional. What if you have a quick tax question or a question about your business? Where can you go without spending a lot of money?

This is why I not only am writing this book, but have also built out my training programs, so you can learn from an expert. The goal with anything that I create is to make it feel like you have a financial planner sitting next to you, guiding you on important money decisions and helping you avoid expensive traps.

I serve millennial professionals, among others, who are trying to learn how to make more money, keep more of their hard-earned money, and grow it for long-term wealth. Whether you're running a business, working as a freelancer, or working in corporate America, there is always room to level up your money game somewhere.

You see, money doesn't have a brain. You have to tell it what to do and where to go. If you don't, it stays stupid. I teach people how to get their money working harder for them. The problem is that most people get overwhelmed with the world of finance or they just don't ever have a good space to talk about it or ask important questions.

There are also land mines to navigate in finance to avoid costly mistakes. This is why we have highly paid financial professionals, of course, but this doesn't mean you can't learn a lot of it yourself. You can, and that's what I teach. I teach you how to be your own financial planner and know when it's time to bring in a professional to help.

This book will guide you through what I call the six puzzle pieces to a complete and healthy financial life. It'll guide you through a similar process that a financial planner would do if you hired them.

- Cash flow management
- Insurance Planning
- Retirement planning
- Investment optimization
- Tax strategy
- Estate/Legacy Planning

Each puzzle piece has two chapters associated with it. I get to the points that you actually NEED to know, and I tell stories of those whom I have worked with (and my own stories) to help you understand these topics better. I will touch on the pitfalls to avoid and show you how to command your money along the way.

I'm confident that by the end of this book you will have obtained new bits of knowledge, some ideas on how you can better position yourself financially going forward, and newfound motivation on what puzzle pieces you need to fit in next in your overall financial plan.

Remember, anyone can learn how to have a healthier and more lucrative financial life. You don't have to be a finance or math whiz, I promise.

Let's dive in!

Part I

Cash Flow Mastery

Chapter 1
Rethinking "Financial Freedom"

The Term "Financial Freedom" Needs a Makeover

"Financial freedom"

These words alone can send some people running for the hills because immediately, they think:

1. Financial freedom can only be achieved by people who make a lot of money.
2. Financial freedom can't be a reality for someone like me because (insert whatever limiting belief here).

Not only that, many people also dismiss conversations about money in any capacity because it's uncomfortable for them to talk about and it stresses them out. I get it; talking about finance isn't as exciting as discussing who got kicked off of the show *The Bachelor*, but a shift is happening that I am excited about.

Talking about money IS becoming less taboo. We're seeing more financial professionals (who actually have credentials) become social media influencers. More "finance-tainment," as they call it, is flooding the internet. I've tried this method myself by doing "Financial Planner Reacts" videos. I comment on bad social media money advice with humor and try to educate people afterward with actual money truths. They have been some of my best performing videos! We also have people publicly displaying how hard they're working to pay off debt and helping people feel less shameful. We're talking about investing more openly. It's beautiful.

As excited as I am about this shift that I see, there is still a lot of work to be done. A lot of people have dipped their toe into finance, interested, but they still feel nervous and uneasy. I hear the concerns from people all the time.

Part of the problem for me when it comes to getting people comfortable with talking about finance lies in the definition of financial freedom.

The classic, old-school definition of "financial freedom" is being able to live off the payments that your investments kick off every year. Maybe you have rental properties, dividend-paying stocks, or interest being paid to you.

However, I can tell you that, after talking with thousands of people, I have learned one major thing: financial freedom is not one-size-fits-all. Everyone who seeks it out has their OWN definition of financial freedom. But we've been force-fed the idea that financial freedom is getting passive payments or a lot of dividends coming in to pay for your lifestyle so that you can sit on a beach sipping piña coladas.

It's time to take the definition of financial freedom out of a box and make it more inclusive so that more people take action to achieve it!

The New "Financial Freedom"

Achieving financial freedom, in my opinion, is being able to eventually live a lifestyle that you love, doing what you enjoy, with money not being a stressor.

So financial freedom is not defined by a specific dollar amount or if you can live off the payments that your investments provide.

With my definition, you can achieve financial freedom while having no cash-flowing investment properties and little to no dividends, while running a business or still working in a career that you love. There really are no limits.

That's probably not what you were told. This may be why you wrote the idea off as unachievable.

Don't get me wrong though; I am all for passive income, dividends, interest, and the like. However, I want people to rethink it a bit and realize success comes in many different forms, and investing strategies run deep! There are so many factors that come into building your plan and a portfolio for your needs. Also, you may have to do something you don't love for a while in order to work toward the life that you do love, and that's okay. It's a process.

Lifestyle goals are the crux of your journey toward financial freedom.

If you have clarity on what type of life you want to live, that is usually the factor that dictates how you handle your money.

So, What Really Is a Lifestyle Goal?

The definition of a "lifestyle goal" is simply how you want to live your life. How do you want to spend your days? Who do you want to spend them with? Where do you want to spend them? It's pretty open ended and there are no right or wrong lifestyle goals.

The strongest example that comes to mind of using lifestyle goals to help you manage your finances is the F.I.R.E. movement (Financial Independence Retire Early). I very much respect the focus and discipline F.I.R.E. members have with their money. Those participating in the F.I.R.E. life are looking to retire way earlier than a traditional age of retirement. They KNOW that they want to retire early, and they invest every dollar that they can while they're young so that they can front-load their investment accounts and not have the obligation to work. They changed their current life (some of them live EXTRAORDINARILY frugally) to achieve their future lifestyle goal of not working at a certain age.

Their lifestyle goal of retiring at an early age usually leads them toward a specific dollar amount goal that defines financial freedom for them.

Will they truly be able to live the life they want and not worry about money? Or will they have to live frugally forever to make the money they saved last for a really long retirement? They won't know until they get to their destination, just like most people, but one thing they do know is what lifestyle goal they're investing for today, and they're making moves. Even if along the way their lifestyle plans change, all that money they're saving and investing will give them something we all want: flexibility.

Destination Unknown

So, what if you have no idea what your lifestyle goals are or what you want, and in turn, can't figure out what your definition of financial freedom is?

If you have no idea what lifestyle you want to live, that's very normal. Most people actually fall into this category. However, it's not necessarily an excuse to NOT try to optimize your finances to work toward something. Goals will always change as we go through life, but we can still make a continuous effort to try to plan, then adjust along the way. Again, wise moves today give you the flexibility that you will need to be able to stay nimble for when that time of clarity does come.

Here is an exercise for you if you're in this camp of uncertainty. Be sure to allow yourself to think freely and dream a little. No limitations (you've probably already limited your thoughts enough).

Step 1: Think about your ***perfect average day*** *if you had all of the money in the world right now.*

- What activities bring you the most joy?
- Where would you physically be in the world?
- Who would you be with, if anyone?
- Are you working?
- Are you volunteering or mentoring?

Step 2: What parts of your perfect average day if you had all of the money in the world are you doing in your current life now?

Step 3: What is it that you think you "can't live without"?

- A life partner?
- A paid-off home? A second home?
- Children?
- Travel?
- A certain hobby or skill set?

- Pets?
- Being near family?
- And so on ...

After going through some thought-provoking questions, it usually helps get you at least to a starting point. Say you can't live without family, for example. In that case, you know that a goal could be retiring near them. This could lead you to a goal of buying a second home close to a parent, for example. Or perhaps you realize you want children one day. Either way, you know that money moves will need to be made now, even if your goal changes.

Don't let the unknown paralyze you. What bad can come of you saving and investing, anyway? You end up with a plump investing account and the ability to be nimble with your life choices.

I wanted to share a few scenarios of people I know who were able to actually achieve their definitions of financial freedom. Two quite different scenarios.

I have an entrepreneur friend who is in his mid-30s and a very free spirit. He has no family yet, and no idea what the future actually looks like for his personal life. But he knows he loves working in his business, and he has hit his goal of being a multi-millionaire in his 30s. He knew his lifestyle goal was owning a business and becoming a millionaire. He didn't know how he was going to get there at first though, but he knew he wanted it. He achieved his definition of financial freedom, and now he is happy with the flexibility he has to shift his lifestyle if he wants to.

I also know someone else who is an older woman in her 60s. She worked in corporate America, and throughout her entire working life, her 401(k) grew to be $500,000. She receives a Social Security check every month and owns a paid-off house. Her only concerns have been wanting to be close to her kids and grandchildren and to be able to pay the bills without worries and take a vacation once a year. She lives a very modest life. She worked hard to pay off her home for retirement, and now her Social Security check covers all of her expenses. She won't have to tap into her retirement except for emergencies or vacations. She has achieved her definition of financial freedom without millions of dollars in the bank.

With proper planning today, even if you're not 100 percent clear on your final destination, you can provide yourself with security and flexibility. Sometimes that can be the lifestyle goal in and of itself. It doesn't have to be super granular, and I hope knowing that financial freedom isn't one-size-fits-all opens you up to thinking about it more deeply.

My goal as you go through this book is to help you get started the right way, with the right mindset.

I want everyone to feel like their definition of financial freedom is within reach.

My husband and I have designed our money life to work for our lifestyle goals. We achieved our definition of financial freedom by our 30s. We worked really hard building businesses in our 20s, strategizing taxes, investing our money, and working toward lives that we love. We don't do things that we hate doing anymore.

We could "retire" to a beach, sipping piña coladas today and never work again, but we wouldn't be happy. We wouldn't be fulfilled, so we keep working in our businesses because it's fun for us. We love sharing our passion for money and investing and helping people.

We even invest based upon our lifestyle goals. We love to travel a lot. So much so that we actually took a trip around the entire world. We always rented our home in the city so that when a lease was up, we could pick up and leave (which we have done multiple times). We don't want to manage real estate investment properties. We tried the real estate flipping game and hated it. We much prefer actively investing in paper assets like stock, or other businesses (including our own). We rent homes in expensive cities (like Austin, Texas) to avoid high real estate prices and high property taxes, and we buy properties and land to own in affordable areas. We have recently bought land in a rural area, full of development potential with much lower housing prices.

My personal investment style gives some people major anxiety! For example, I have friends who would much prefer to own a portfolio of real estate over stocks.

Everyone is different. We invest for our lifestyle, and that's okay!

The Real Problem with More People Achieving Financial Freedom

Let's shift and talk about wealth inequality for a moment. It's a big issue in this country, but I tend to think that a big part of the problem is truly a lack of financial education. We're not taught how to properly manage our finances in school, and we may not have had parents who taught us either. As I have gone through my own journey, I learn of many people who really don't know what they're doing with their money; even some people with millions of dollars in the bank don't really know what they're doing.

This is why financial planners and advisors have very high-paying jobs. The world of money confuses people to the core, so they outsource it to someone else and pay the big bucks for it. But most people can't afford a financial advisor, or they don't have enough assets for one to even want to talk to them (this is beginning to change, but it's still costly for most people). The internet is our savior, and it has made financial advice more accessible to people, but I've also seen a load of bad financial advice out there. Not to call out any names, but I've even seen finance "gurus" who are very famous with huge followings give terrible financial and investing advice.

One problem has been that the people who SHOULD be teaching finance, being the Certified Public Accountants, the Certified Financial Planners, and the investment advisors, are usually busy making money in their firms and don't have time to educate the masses. But the good news is that internet marketing is becoming an essential part of a financial professional's success. Putting out sound, free professional advice through social media is the new way to get clients. It's almost impossible now to start a firm without doing this to some degree, unless you have a really tight and reliable network.

So, I think the direction we are heading is a good one overall. The more professionals who are out there giving financial tips and tricks, the better. In fact, I encourage you to find these professionals with financial credentials and follow them. They give out amazing and useful content that many people have normally had to pay big bucks for.

Back to Your Money Story

I suggest thinking back about your money story, like we talked about in the Introduction. What shaped you? What did you learn or not learn? Is any part of your money story holding you back from achieving more in your financial life? Maybe you just need a fresh take on what "financial freedom" means to make it feel more accessible?

Define what financial freedom looks like to you now. Know that it will change, but this is your starting point. You may not know your final destination, but that doesn't mean you can't work toward financial flexibility for when you DO gain more clarity.

You can start to make REAL change in your financial life. You can start investing, building businesses, saving for your child's future, working toward early retirement, and more. You can start feeling more purpose behind every money move that you make and have clarity on how it will get you to your definition of financial freedom.

Journal:

What is your definition of financial freedom? Think back to your *perfect average day*.

Chapter 2
Cash Flow Power Moves

In the last chapter, I covered why the term "financial freedom" needs a makeover. I walked you through an exercise to help you gather some lifestyle goals. Remember that it all starts with lifestyle goals.

Now we get into an important topic. What to actually *do* with your money!

"I Don't Really Know What to Do with My Money"

Having money doesn't mean you know how to manage money well. It's a big misconception. You know how to EARN money but not necessarily how to MANAGE IT.

I have seen people with multi-millions of dollars not properly managing their money. It's in a checking account, earning no interest, not keeping pace with inflation, and with no plan in sight. (Hint: There are much more strategic places to put millions of dollars, and we will talk more on inflation in the investing chapter!)

The truth is, no matter how much money you make or have in the bank, money management is a skill set EVERYONE needs ... no matter what. It shouldn't be reserved just for financial professionals or wealthy people. You don't have to know all the nitty-gritty details, but a foundation is essential and empowering.

Most people simply don't know what to really do with their dollars. It can be an overwhelming feeling trying to figure out if you should pay down debts, spend it on a vacation, invest more, or just put it into savings. Or people may be afraid to do anything at all because they don't like change, or they don't want to take on any risk.

But not taking mindful action, or taking no action at all, could be the riskiest thing you ever do.

I've seen people across all earning spectrums have different ways of handling their money. It's one of those funny things where you can see someone making $50,000 a year have more free cash to save and invest than someone making $500,000 a year. This is why I tell people that they shouldn't feel like they can't have a plan of action or that there is simply nothing to do because they don't have a large amount of money.

There is always something you can do to better manage your money, no matter how much of it you have (or don't have).

Financial Freedom Is the Goal; Cash Flow Is the Vehicle to Get You There

Achieving your definition of financial freedom begins with having positive cash flow. Cash flow is your money left over after paying your expenses.

Income - Taxes - Expenses = Cash Flow (and you want this to be a positive number)

In this chapter we will be covering what I call "cash flow clarity," the biggest pitfalls when it comes to cash flow, and how to actually make sure your cash flow is going to the right places. The end goal is to know what purpose every dollar is serving for your life.

Cash Flow Clarity: In Your Sight, In Your Mind

You know that cash flow is the vehicle that gets you to your definition of financial freedom.

So, do you have cash flow clarity?

To recap, cash flow is the amount of money you have left over from your income after you pay your taxes, living expenses, entertainment, and whatever else your lifestyle requires. We want money coming in to be greater than money going out. It's a pretty simple concept that most people tend to understand at surface level.

However, I have worked with many clients who struggle with "cash flow clarity."

Cash flow clarity is knowing how much money you'll have to actually allocate to your different "goal buckets" and financial needs. Cash flow allocation is essentially where your "money management" skills kick in.

When I ask those who struggle with where their money goes, or if they've tracked it, the answer is almost always "I don't track it, so I'm not really sure."

We juggle a lot in our lives. Tracking your money is another thing to add to the long to-do list, and for most people it goes on the back burner. Or maybe the picture isn't that pretty after all of those Uber Eats orders, and it's easier to play the "out of sight, out of mind" game. But I promise you, "in my sight, in my mind" needs to be your motto. If you don't track your health, or track your business performance, or track if you have household essentials in your house, what happens? Your health may decline, your business performance may lag, or you may run out of toilet paper at the worst time!

Tracking your income and spending is essential if you want to live a rich money life. Keeping your situation top of mind helps you make essential changes like cutting back on spending or taking that extra freelancing job so that you can get your cash flow higher. On the flip side, awareness may even help you realize you've got very healthy cash flow and you need to direct more money to the right places more efficiently (again, those money management skills kicking in!).

So, cash flow clarity is the first step to better finances. You have to know what you're working with.

The Rich Get Richer, and the Poor Get Poorer

Debt is a cash flow killer. I'm not talking about your home mortgage, or even most student loans (these tend to have lower interest rates). I am talking about the really bad stuff: high-interest debts like credit cards and personal loans.

Debt works against people to keep them poor just as quickly as people who invest their money get richer. There is a reason why people who are in debt feel like they'll never get out of it and why people who are on the opposite side—and investing—feel like wealth comes fairly easily. It's called compounding interest that either works for you (via investing) or against you (via holding debts, particularly high-interest debts).

Compound interest is defined simply as "interest earned on interest." Here is an example:

If you have $1,000 in a savings account in year 1, and you earn 10% interest in that year, you earn $100 in interest in year 1.

Then, in year 2, your starting balance is $1,100. You earn the same 10% in year 2, but instead of the 10% being calculated on $1,000, it's calculated on $1,100. So you earn $110 in year 2 in interest.

Interest rate: 10%

Starting Balance	*Interest Earned*	*End Balance*
Year 1: $1,000	*$100*	*$1,100*
Year 2: $1,100	*$110*	*$1,210*
Year 3: $1,210	*$121*	*$1,331*

This continues over and over again ... it's like a snowball, and it either works for you as an investor or against you as a high-interest debt holder (looking at your credit cards).

Here is an example of the major difference of being an investor versus a debt holder:

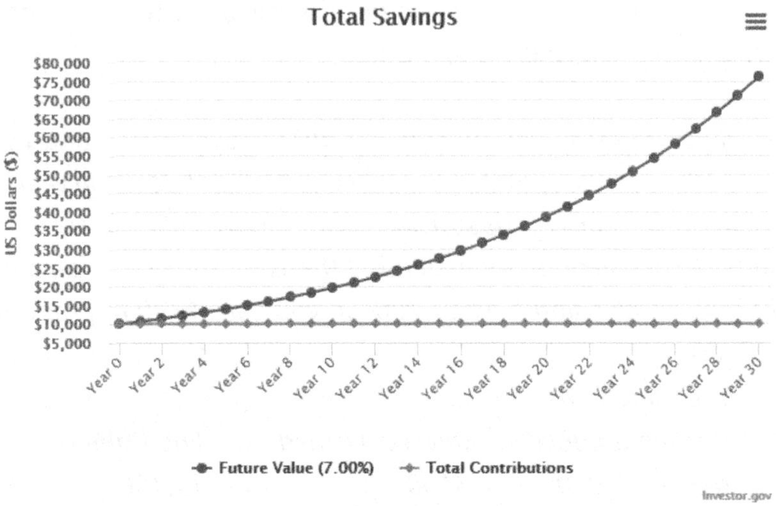

Investing $10,000, earning 7% return annually for 30 years

You see how your one-time $10,000 contribution turns into over $75,000 over time by investing?

Now imagine adding regular contributions monthly or yearly, helping your balances grow even more (which most people do via their retirement plans). This is how the rich get richer—by funneling cash flow into investments that provide returns that compound year after year.

Holding high-interest debt at 14.52% interest paying the minimum payment of 3%

Assuming you only pay a minimum payment of 3% of the balance, with the average credit card interest rate of 14.52%, it will take you 19 years to pay off the $10,000 when making only the minimum payment ... and you would end up paying roughly $6,600 in interest.

So the interest paid alone as a percentage of the original debt will be 66% of the original $10,000 balance. That $10,000 debt ended up costing you $16,600 and a lot of precious money that you could have been investing instead.

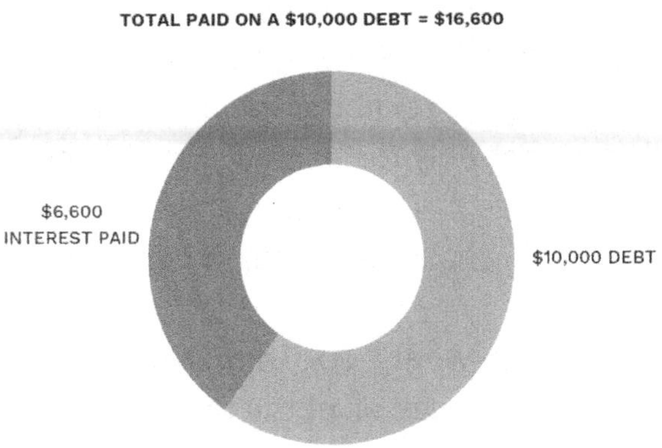

Source: She Talks Finance

This concept alone, I feel, is under-taught to young people. If people could visually see how the spending and debt they take on will affect their cash flow and, in turn, their entire financial life (it's all connected), I think things could look different for a lot of people. Imagine if we knew what every dollar we spend frivolously could compound into if we invested it instead. Or if we visually saw a graph on our credit card statements showing how long it's actually going to take to pay our balances off based on our payments. It may make a person not make that extra purchase, or they may opt for the less expensive option next time.

Education around how compound interest works and the other things you CAN do with money is enough to change behaviors.

I was teaching a class about investing and retirement accounts, and we were making vision boards in class to help people manifest their money goals and dreams.

I got to chatting with a young mother who was in the class, and she was telling me about how she had a shopping addiction, and she was in debt because of it. She couldn't stop buying shoes, clothes, and purses that she didn't need. She continued to tell me how the class I was teaching had opened her eyes to her actions, and she realized she had to make a change not only for herself, but for her children as well. I got a message from her several months later. She had kicked the shopping habit and paid off her debts and wanted to thank me!

That is why I do what I do. That is why I am preaching education and knowledge all of the time.

Sometimes I am taken by surprise at how I think people may not find my content or education impactful enough, but then I realize that there are many people like this woman, and we can make a big difference with education.

Perfection Is Not the Goal

Spending money feels good. I admit "retail therapy" is real. I am guilty of feeling stressed and going to buy something nice for myself to try to feel better. (Nobody is perfect.) But perfection isn't the goal. Simply getting better is the goal.

I often see people with negative cash flow, who know they shouldn't spend money on frivolous things, doing it anyway.

It's no different from wanting to get fit and lose weight but eating a piece of cake while staring at the high calorie count on the label. You know it's full of sugar and calories. You know it won't get you to your fitness goals, but it tastes good, and you don't care. Emotions take over. This happens day in and day out with people's finances in many different ways. People sabotage their own financial well-being. It can relate to frivolous spending, buying insurance products that they don't need, taking unnecessary loans from their 401(k) because of not having an emergency fund, not doing any tax planning, and more.

Once someone who wants to lose weight gets fed up enough with looking in the mirror, they start to change. They start exercising, eating better, and seeing the weight come off. Seeing the progress is what motivates them to keep going. Do they want the chocolate cake slice they're used to having regularly? Yes, but they know it'll prevent them from seeing progress, so they say no more, in return for progress in losing weight.

It then becomes a lifestyle.

This is how it works with your money. Once you see progress in the form of a higher savings account balance, less debt, dividends, and investment accounts growing, it becomes a lifestyle.

When it comes to spending, I try to encourage clients to ask themselves two questions before purchasing something that they're not sure about:

1. "Do I really need this [insert thing]?"
2. "Is this money better served somewhere else?"

That, at least, gets you thinking before sliding the card.

You Can Only Budget So Much

Budgeting and living within your means is the most common way to increase your cash flow.

However, you can only budget so much. Eventually, you reach a wall where you've cut as much as you can, and you just can't cut any more. Not only that, but budgeting is not fun, and most people won't stick to it.

Unfortunately for all of us, without positive cash flow, our finances are dead in the water. Simple as that.

So, sometimes, you have to get more proactive, and you have to go seek out places where you can find more money.

Here are some ways you can increase your cash flow:

1. **Take on a side gig.** Today's gig economy makes it pretty easy to do this. Websites like Upwork.com or Fiverr.com have given many people the ability to find extra work across a long list of job descriptions and skill sets. Delivery apps like Uber, DoorDash, or Instacart have opened up a way for people to earn extra cash by delivering food and groceries.
2. **Resell goods.** I have a friend who created Ralli Roots, (https://www.ralliroots.com), a million-dollar reselling business, with just a couple hundred dollars, buying goods at thrift stores and garage sales, then reselling them on a website like eBay for a profit. Start with selling things around your house that you don't need anymore.
3. **Get a roommate or downsize your home.** I know, if you're living alone, it's hard to try living with somebody else, but it can make a huge impact on increasing your cash flow. Also, it doesn't have to be forever.
4. **Get rid of an expensive vehicle.** I have seen car payments as a very high percentage of people's income. If this is you, consider nixing the expensive car and choosing something more economical.

5. **Ask for a raise.** Don't be afraid to ask your employer what you're worth. Go in with a strong case of how you've improved operations at your company and the value that you add. Bring in data if you have it to help your case. This is one of the greatest ways to increase cash flow.
6. **Turn a hobby into a side business.** Are you creative? With websites like Etsy.com, you're able to sell goods pretty easily. People love handmade goods!
7. **Consult.** Are you an expert in something? Software? Websites? Video editing? Writing? Marketing? Design? Productivity? Bookkeeping? You can literally get paid to consult with other businesses or business owners to help them get better at your skill set. With Shopify or Square, it's easy to set up a business website and take payments.
8. **Optimize your taxes.** Try to find tax savings if you're a business owner or freelancer (more on that later!).

As I say, cash flow is QUEEN. It's the ultimate goal to have positive cash flow in your life (your income is more than your expenses), because this gives you incredible options to enable you to design the life that you truly want.

The sooner you free up your money, the sooner you can start to make REAL change in your financial life. You can start investing, building businesses, saving for your child's future, working toward early retirement, and more.

Where Should the Cash Flow Go?

Acquiring cash is half the battle ... then you have to tell your cash what to do.

I know that we're all human, and life doesn't always go according to plan. Sometimes a big, unexpected bill comes in that you can't pay, or your hours get cut back at work, or you have to help a family member get out of a bind. It's life, and it happens. This is why the rest of this book will be important. You'll learn how to plan to prepare for whatever life may throw at you.

But I wanted to give a general three-step overview of where your cash flow should actually go first, because I do see a lot of people approach this with no real strategy.

1. ***The first step in any cash flow allocation plan is to make sure your emergency fund is fully funded.***

An emergency fund is money set aside for things like job loss, being out of work due to a health condition, or having to stop working to care for a loved one. The emergency fund functions as your bucket of money to pay your essential bills to survive. The amount of money that should be in your emergency fund is anywhere from three to six months of living expenses typically.

Here is my advice though; everyone has different risk tolerance and different life scenarios. I say to throw out the "typical 3–6 month" rule for a moment, and set an emergency fund amount that makes you feel secure and comfortable when considering your personal situation. If you run a business, or have inconsistent income, you may need as much as a 12-month emergency fund to feel comfortable. If you're living with family or have the ability to, and you know you'll have a roof over your head and food no matter what happens, maybe your fund can be just a few months. It's very personal!

Consider what will help you sleep best at night.

2. ***The second step in cash flow allocation is paying down high-interest debt.***

If you have a lot of high-interest debts like credit cards or some personal loans, the interest will compound against you and most likely negate any type of investing you do. That is why this step is so important to prioritize. I consider high-interest debt to be anything over 7%, but this is debatable among financial professionals. So this will not include things like your mortgage or other lower interest loans (just keep paying on those as normal—no need to have low interest debts paid off to move to step 3). If you're torn between saving for your emergency fund and paying debt, you will want to be working on paying these two simultaneously. If you go straight to paying off the debts without any emergency fund, you are setting yourself up to have to charge more high-interest debt if an emergency does come about.

I see people all of the time trying to go straight to investing before tackling #1 and #2. The issue here is your gains from investing could be wiped out plus some from the interest that you pay on your high-interest debts.

If you're earning an average annual return in the market of 10%, but you're paying 20% interest on your debts, you're losing overall on a percentage basis.

You may be thinking to yourself, *But Nikki, I get a match on my 401(k) contributions at work, and those are invested ... should I continue to do this?*

The answer is yes. Contribute just enough to your company retirement plan to get the match. Why? Because a match is free money. That's a 100% return on your investment! Again, only contribute enough to get the match; then when your debts are paid off and your emergency fund is set, you can start ramping more money into your retirement accounts or other investments.

3. ***The third step in a cash flow allocation plan is to start investing more.***

You have your emergency fund, and you have your high-interest debts paid off; now it's time to ramp up your investing machine. You can work toward maxing out retirement plan contributions, investing in a taxable account to take advantage of long-term capital gains, investing in your business, and more. We will have a few chapters dedicated to investing in more detail.

Again, this is a general three-step process to better cash flow allocation. There may be nuances to your personal situation, and there are steps in between the steps, but the deeper you get into this book, the more skills you'll learn to help you fine-tune your strategy.

Are You Ready to ... Finance?

Okay, we have some basics out of the way. Now it's time to move into the nuts and bolts of an ironclad money plan.

I like to call the rest of this book "the fun stuff." Next, we move into insurance.

I know what you're thinking ... *Nikki, that sounds super boring.*

But what if I told you insurance you don't have (or insurance you have that you don't need) could cause you and your family big financial trouble? That's worth reading further, I think.

So let's keep this train running and move into optimizing the next part of your plan.

Journal:

It's important to have clarity on your income and expenses in order to move forward managing your money better. Take this time to review your finances and write down how much cash flow you have at the end of the month (or year, if you have sporadic income).

Income – Taxes – Expenses = Cash Flow

____

____

____

What are some things you can do to increase your cash flow?

____

____

____

____

____

Part II

The Art Of Insurance Planning

Chapter 3
Safeguarding Your Entire Life

We have now covered cash flow, which we know is super important for reaching our financial goals, but now it's time to look at one of the less sexy topics in personal finance ... insurance.

There is a way to determine how insurance can fit into your financial plan, and we're going to dive into the different types of insurance and how to know what you really need (and really don't need).

One unforeseen event can destroy someone's financial health ... insurance can play a big role in helping you prevent that from happening.

Insurance Is Just Another Expense ... Until You Really Need It

I know what you're thinking: *Nikki, can we get to the fun stuff like making money with investing? Insurance is boooooring.*

I hear you ... insurance is one of those subjects that most people prefer to glance over, with little attention to details, or many feel they can get by in life without certain types of insurance. But the truth is you don't think you need insurance or more insurance, until you REALLY need it.

I actually was an insurance claims adjuster for a large insurance company for many years, so I got an interesting peek into this world. I handled medical and property damage claims for car accidents. I talked to hundreds of people over my career, and I learned a lot about how many people either don't have proper coverage or don't have enough of it for hard times.

Unfortunately, as a claims adjuster, you're on the other end of that phone having to tell someone, "Sorry, we can't pay to get your car repaired because you were at fault and didn't have collision coverage on your vehicle."

Or, even worse, listening to that same person cry after learning they have no rental car coverage and not enough money saved, and now they have no way to get their car repaired OR get to work (yes, this is a true story—it happens every day).

It's disheartening, because there is nothing that can be done by that time for these people. Like I said, you don't know you need it until you REALLY need it!

There are many types of insurance, and not everyone needs all of the varieties of it. We will cover insurance types in more detail in the next chapter. For this chapter, I will be walking you through how to link insurance needs to your definition of financial freedom, with the following in mind.

- The definition of risk is the possibility of suffering harm or loss; danger.
- Risk is everywhere, in every aspect of our lives.
- Perils are events that actually cause harm or loss, like a hurricane or flood, for example.

Our daily habits carry risks, for example:

- What we ingest in our bodies, whether it's food or vices like alcohol or cigarettes, can be risky to our health.
- Going most places carries the risk of getting sick or contracting a certain kind of disease.
- Our hobbies (like skiing) or our jobs (like working in construction) may carry risk. You could easily get hurt or even break a bone.
- Our need to commute and get around town carries risk of being in a car accident.
- Inclement weather, or crummy thieves or vandals, can cause damage to our property.
- Sudden, unexpected illness or death can happen for anyone at any time.
- We are even susceptible to lawsuits that could take away our hard-earned money and assets.

Not to be a drag, but living life is, essentially, living with risk. But we can't live in a suit of bubble wrap—in fear and not living our lives the way we want to, right?

This is why insurance was created: so that we can have the ability to pay someone else to take on the consequences of risks that exist in our lives.

So, how do you actually reconcile how insurance fits into your plan, budget, and definition of financial freedom?

First, let's cover the main types of insurance and some basic definitions. (We will go into more detail in the next chapter.)

There Is Insurance for Everything

The main types of insurance and what they may cover:

- **Vehicle** – Covers damage to your vehicle, liability if you're at fault for an accident, and medical expenses
- **Health** – Covers medical expenses
- **Home** – Covers damage to your home and property
- **Life** – Pays money to your designated beneficiary upon your death
- **Disability** – Pays a certain percentage of your income if you are unable to work or run your business
- **Annuity** – Insurance contracts that promise to pay you regular income either immediately or in the future
- **Liability** – Covers you if you are involved in a lawsuit
- **Business** – Covers property in your business, liability for property damage or bodily injury, and more

Definitions to know:

- **Deductible** – A specific dollar amount that you will have to pay before your insurance pays
- **Self-Insure** – Not purchasing an insurance policy with the intention of paying for any incident costs
- **Policy Limit** – The maximum amount a policy will pay out for an incident
- **Elimination Period** – The amount of time you may have to wait to receive any payment from the insurance company (common with disability policies, and why an emergency fund is helpful here)

So, now that we have some basics out of the way, it's time to ask yourself a few questions to figure out where you stand with your needs for insurance.

First, you need to determine these things:

1. **How much exposure to risk do you have in your daily life?**
   a) How often do you drive a car?
   b) How often do you do risky activities/sports?
   c) Where does your property exist? Is it a common location for natural disasters or theft?
   d) Are you more susceptible to certain medical conditions?
2. **How much savings do you have?**
   a) Are you willing to put your savings at risk of an unknown and unexpected expense like medical bills or a big vehicle repair bill after a car accident?
3. **How much would each incident (health, disability, theft, death, and so on) impact your financial picture?**
   a) Do you have family who will be impacted, or is it just you?
   b) Will you be able to financially support yourself and your family until you can get a hold of insurance payouts?
   c) Do you have a lot of assets at risk of lawsuits?

Next, you need to answer these questions:

1. **Which types of risk do I want to self-insure by paying for expenses out of pocket, and which types of risk do I want to transfer to an insurance company to cover in case of an incident?**
2. **What is the best deductible that will complement my cash flow and emergency fund?**
    a) Deductibles can range from zero dollars to thousands of dollars depending on the type of insurance.
3. **Does the insurance coverage make sense for my situation?**
    a) Example 1: If you have nobody you need to leave money to when you pass, why would you carry life insurance?
    b) Example 2: If you're healthy and don't go to the doctor often, do you need the most expensive and comprehensive health insurance plan?

So, as you can see, there is a lot to consider, and the decision of which type of insurance and how large a policy you need is a bit nuanced.

You shouldn't be buying insurance policies willy-nilly. You want to really put some thought into your needs and how much money you're willing to spend to protect yourself and your family.

Back to Your Definition of Financial Freedom

The goal is to be able to reach your definition of financial freedom. Insurance can actually play a larger part in this than you'd think!

Why? Because a perilous event can have serious financial consequences. Of course, this is what your emergency fund is for, right? It's there to cover you for whatever amount of time you saved up for. But some incidents (usually, the unforeseen ones) can be more costly than your emergency fund can provide for.

There is no way to know everything that will happen in one's life; this is why we reduce our risk with things like insurance planning.

Here's an example scenario:

Let's say you're on track with your savings and investing goals, and everything is going great as long as you continue to work and make an income. You then find out that you have a medical condition that will require surgery and you will not be able to work for six months due to the recovery. You have no short-term disability insurance and no one to help you out.

What do you do? You're likely going to have to use your entire emergency fund if you have one, take on debt, or tap into your precious investing account to survive. What does that do? It puts a dent in your plan and pushes you back a little further.

So, how else could a situation like this have played out? Well, let's say you had short-term disability insurance. The insurance pays 70% of your income if you can't perform any type of work, and you only have an elimination period of two weeks to wait to receive your first weekly payment.

That changes things quite a bit there. Not only is this money tax-free if you paid all of the policy premiums (and if your payment is based on gross income, it may equate to actually replacing a large percentage of your take-home pay), but you may also not end up having to use your entire emergency fund or having to touch your investment accounts.

I personally know someone who was in this situation. The difference is, he had no savings and lived paycheck to paycheck, but the short-term disability payment was always paid. Turns out he had to have surgery and couldn't work for months. The disability insurance payments he received to supplement his income saved him, big time.

Now, will most people end up paying more in premiums than what the insurance company pays out to them on claims? Yes, likely. That's the insurance game. But it's up to you to decide which risks you're willing to take and which perils you want to be protected from.

Everyone's financial picture is quite different. Maybe you're fortunate enough to have a very healthy savings buffer and you can self-insure multiple risks with no problems. For example, maybe you'll be okay for a while if you can't work due to illness and have no need to purchase a disability policy.

Let us remember the "personal" in personal finance.

Are Insurance Salespeople Bad?

Insurance salespeople have really developed a bad reputation over the years, particularly with life and annuity insurance.

Not everyone selling insurance is bad, though. Most are actually trying to do good by their clients, and insurance is a much-needed product for many people. But a little education goes a long way when it comes to working with an insurance agent. It could save you THOUSANDS of dollars over your policy's life, or help you avoid buying an unneeded policy altogether.

With that said, every day, a financial planner sheds a tear over the terrible annuity contract that their client got suckered into buying from some salesperson before they could look at it. Maybe it had a ton of fees, or maybe the client didn't even need it.

For years, the insurance industry was all about selling complex and, might I say, predatory policies that clients couldn't even understand, all to line salespeople's pockets with commissions.

Although this is still happening, and there are still some pretty complex life and annuity policies being sold to people, we're seeing customers become more aware of these tactics, and they're asking more questions.

My goal in the next chapter is to explain some of these policies in more detail, point out the things you should be looking out for, and show you how to determine if you even need the policy so you can be a more informed buyer.

The main goal is to balance the cost of premiums with the coverage that satisfies your needs—and nothing more.

Journal:

What risks in life worry you the most?

Chapter 4
Decoding Insurance and Finding the Best Policy

In the last chapter we covered how to tell where insurance can fit into your financial plan.

In this chapter we will dive into the details of the different types of insurance and what to look for when shopping for them.

Remember, the goal is to balance the cost of insurance with coverage that satisfies your needs.

There's a Policy for That … but Don't Get Trapped

Insurance across the board is actually pretty customizable. You can take away or add coverage, or tinker with deductibles to change the cost of the insurance. A lot of people tend to do this when trying to get an insurance payment that they think they can manage to pay comfortably.

However, you don't want to do too much tinkering to the point where the most important coverages get removed or reduced, especially with auto or homeowners insurance.

That's the trick. You don't want to end up in a situation like we talked about in the last chapter, where one day you really end up needing coverage that you just don't have.

Start with Your Assets in Mind ...

First things first, with insurance planning, it helps to have a list of the value of your assets and your liabilities (we also call this your personal balance sheet). Your balance sheet shows you what you have and what you need to be protecting or planning around, so it's important!

Here is an example of a balance sheet that would outline a person's or family's assets and liabilities owed:

Your Name		Year
Assets		**Fair Market Value $**
Current assets:		Current Year
Checking Account	$	10,000.00
Savings Account	$	15,000.00
Certificate of Deposit	$	5,000.00
Total current assets	$	30,000.00
Fixed assets:		Current Year
Primary Home	$	250,000.00
Jewelry	$	5,000.00
Vehicle	$	20,000.00
Antiques/Collectibles	$	1,000.00
Total fixed assets	$	276,000.00
Other assets:		Current Year
Taxable Brokerage	$	1,000.00
IRA	$	3,000.00
401(k)	$	10,000.00
Total other assets	$	14,000.00
Total assets	**$**	**320,000.00**
Liabilities and owner's equity		**Fair Market Value**
Current liabilities:		Current Year
Credit Card	$	5,000.00
Personal Loan	$	1,000.00
Vehicle Loan	$	15,000.00
Student Loan	$	10,000.00
Total current liabilities	$	31,000.00
Long-term liabilities:		Current Year
Mortgage	$	200,000.00
Total long-term liabilities	$	200,000.00
Total liabilities and owner's equity	**$**	**231,000.00**
Balance	**$**	**89,000.00**

Source: She Talks Finance

Side note: You want to update your balance sheet every year so that you can keep track of your net worth. It can be a motivating factor to getting debts paid or funneling more money into investment accounts to grow.

The next tip in insurance planning is to find an independent insurance agent if you're going to work with one. A financial planner may also help connect you to a trusted agent. Why an independent agent? They can find you the best policy by shopping multiple insurance companies versus working with an agent who only works for one company. You know, "Joe from State Farm"? He is not independent; he works for State Farm and will only sell policies from State Farm. That is the difference.

If you know a trusted agent who works for a particular insurance company, that is fine, but if not, an independent agent can be pretty nice to have. Also, don't be afraid to ask questions—a lot of them! Some types of insurance, life insurance and annuities in particular, can get complex, so depending on the type of policy it is, ask about the policy premiums, fees, riders, surrender charges, and more.

Policy fees are annual costs that the insurance company charges you to keep the policy in force. They may be administrative fees for certain types of life insurance or annuities.

Policy riders are added benefits that you can add to your policy for an extra premium that you'd have to pay. An example of this could be a rider to a homeowners insurance policy that covers an expensive piece of jewelry not covered by your policy limits.

Surrender charges are typically for life insurance or annuity contracts, and they are a cost to cancel the policy and cash in your money. These can be very punitive, so you want to make sure you're aware of them.

The Main Types of Insurance That You May Need

I have listed these in order of how common they are ... but remember, you may or may not need one of these depending on your personal situation and the assets you own.

Consider how expensive an accident of any kind would be for you and your family when helping you figure out what kind of insurance and how much you should get. Keep in mind that auto accidents, health emergencies, home or property damage, and death can all have expensive consequences. So, it's difficult to say that there is an order of importance here. It depends on your situation.

Also, keep in mind that some insurance agents are licensed to sell multiple types of insurance, and some only do one type of insurance. You'll also need to find an agent licensed in your state to sell you insurance. I suggest using online reviews, or asking someone you know for a referral, and calling around to talk to a few to find one you like.

Auto Insurance

This may be one of your most important insurance policies simply because most of us are driving on the road almost every day, which increases the likelihood of an accident of some kind happening.

When choosing the details of your auto insurance policy, consider a few things:

1. What is the value of your car? Do you want to save money on premiums and pay out of pocket for possible

damages, or the other way around? Would a large repair or medical bill be an issue?

2. Can your savings or cash flow pay for deductibles if needed? You may be able to handle higher deductibles if you have enough cash to cover them, reducing your premiums.
3. Accidents and tickets can really drive up insurance costs. Do your best to keep a clean driving record!

As some of you reading may have already experienced in your life, a car accident can be very, very expensive. Not only that, you're also open to major liability if you are at fault for a serious accident and don't have policy limits to cover damage and injury. On the flip side of this, you can't control what policy limits other drivers carry on their policies, if any active insurance at all!

This is where coverage types like "uninsured/underinsured motorist" come in. Don't overlook them.

Throughout your life, auto insurance will likely be your most-used insurance. It's important to evaluate your policy to make sure it's comprehensive and that deductible amounts are manageable for your financial situation.

Health Insurance

There are entire books on health insurance alone ... so I won't be able to go into as much detail here, but I want to give you some tips and tricks for finding a policy that works for you.

You can purchase health insurance from a licensed health insurance agent. They need to be licensed in the state that you live in, in order to sell you insurance. These agents can be very helpful for finding you the right policy ... so I suggest giving it a try! Agents are also in the know regarding government policies that help you save money on the cost of premiums.

Health insurance coverage runs far and wide, with all types of services covered, or not covered, multiple sizes of deductibles, and more.

Here are some considerations when choosing coverage:

1. How often do you go to the doctor? Are you a frequent user of coverage, with regular doctor and specialist appointments? The more you plan to use the coverage, the more it may make sense to pay for the policy richer in benefits.
2. Add up all of your medical bills, copays, and prescriptions for the prior year. Compare coverage of your bills on other policies to be sure you're on the right one and that your premium payments make sense in relation to your use of the policy. You will also want to do this to see if you may be able to downgrade coverage and save money on premiums, while holding enough coverage for a catastrophic event and routine maintenance.
3. If you're a low user of insurance, a high-deductible plan coupled with a Health Savings Account (HSA) may make a lot of sense. These accounts are underrated. You can not only get a tax deduction for your HSA contributions, but you can also pay for qualified medical expenses tax-free throughout your life. You can also invest the funds in your HSA into the market if you don't plan to use them (and they get to grow tax-deferred). The HSA essentially turns into a regular IRA account at the age of 65 with no penalty for

non-medical withdrawals, while keeping the tax-free benefit for qualified medical expenses for your life.

4. Think ahead. If you are expecting to have a baby or to have a certain surgery, consider adjusting your coverage far enough in advance so that you don't get caught off-guard.

Can't afford health insurance? You're not alone. Unfortunately, many Americans go without coverage due to the cost of insurance, even after tax credits are applied to marketplace plans. We're hoping to see better healthcare reform in the future to make care more accessible. A health insurance agent can help you navigate the marketplace plans and figure out if you'll qualify for a tax credit to make it more affordable.

Here are some tips in the meantime:

1. Be sure to ask your doctors about whether they can reduce your bills for your having to pay out of pocket. Otherwise, as an out-of-pocket payer, you may end up paying the same amount for a doctor visit as someone with a high-deductible plan.
2. You may be able to take an itemized tax deduction if your medical expenses become a large percentage of your income. Be aware of this for the future (tax laws are always subject to change).

Homeowners Insurance

For most homeowners, your home is your most expensive personal asset. Yet homeowners insurance coverage often gets overlooked or under-analyzed.

Repairing damage to a home can be exceptionally expensive. Also, most insurance policies contain a provision that if you're not properly covered for at least 80% of the replacement cost value of your home (excluding the land, as land is not covered), your insurance company may not pay out on a claim for the full amount.

The best rule of thumb? Make sure your homeowners policy covers 100% of the replacement cost value of your dwelling.

Homeowners insurance, like any other insurance, is shoppable so that you can find the best deal. Also, many insurance companies will offer discounts if you bundle multiple types of insurance policies with them (auto, home, boat, renters, and so forth). So you'll want to check your policy every year and make sure you're happy with the coverage you're getting for your premium and see if there are any discounts you can qualify for (especially if you add something like an alarm system to your home).

Homeowners policies may vary in terms of type of coverage depending on the type of home that is being insured. For example, a condo policy will differ in a few ways from a single family home policy. You may also get a renters policy that works like a homeowners policy to cover your belongings.

Most homeowners policies will have open peril coverage with certain exclusions that won't be covered, like earthquake, flood, neglect, war, nuclear hazard, power failure, and intentional loss. You may have to get additional coverage for natural disasters if you live in an area prone to them.

When digging into your policy, you'll want to be sure your coverage is sufficient for:

- **Your Dwelling -** This covers your actual main residence and anything attached to it like a garage. You want to be sure to insure 100% of the replacement value cost of your dwelling.
- **Other Structures -** This covers replacing or repairing small detached structures on the dwelling property, such as a shed, up to a certain limit.
- **Personal Property -** This covers your personal belongings in your home up to certain limits. You'll want to be sure the limits are sufficient to cover your most prized possessions. There are often very low limits on things like jewelry, firearms, or furs that you may need to purchase separate coverage for. Also, keep cash that you have in your home in a water- or fire-proof bag, as limits on replacing cash are usually very low on policies.
- **Personal Liability -** This covers, up to certain limits, bodily injury or property damages that you or resident family members are legally liable for either on or off of the covered premises.

Disability Insurance

Got a very physically demanding job? Or are you a skilled professional, like a dentist or a surgeon, who relies heavily on the function of a certain body part, like your hands? Worried that loss of work due to a health event or accident will really put you back financially? If so, disability insurance may make a lot of sense.

According to the Social Security Administration, the probability of disability during our prime working years is actually higher than death.

So it's interesting how we usually plan more for death than we do for disability (ideally, you want to plan for both).

There are three main things to be aware of with disability insurance:

1. **The definition of disability**
   a) Own occupation – You can't work in your own occupation due to your disability. The definition found in this type of policy describes a threshold that is easier to meet; therefore, the premiums are more expensive. This is the more desirable coverage.
   b) Any occupation – You can't work in any occupation at all due to your disability. This definition describes a more difficult threshold to meet as there is likely some job you're capable of doing; therefore, the premiums are less expensive.
2. **The elimination period (time you have to wait to receive your first payment)**
   a) The longer the elimination period, the less expensive the premium.
   b) The shorter the elimination period, the more expensive the premium.
   c) Consider how soon you'll need to get ahold of money once you become disabled.

3. **The percentage of salary covered and coverage period**
    a) What percentage of your salary will the policy cover? Is it based on gross or net pay?
    b) How long will benefits be paid? This period is also known as your coverage period. Short-term policies will cover you up to a few years, and long-term policies will cover you potentially up to retirement age.

Life Insurance

Life insurance can provide great peace of mind and actually have multiple benefits to an overall financial plan like tax-deferral growth. However, not everyone actually needs it.

Here are some main points relevant to deciding if life insurance is for you:

1. **Do you have a need for life insurance?**
    a) Do you have a family or individuals who depend on you monetarily?
        i) How much money would they need to pay bills, put kids through college, pay for your burial, pay off a home, take care of loved ones with a disability, and whatever else is important to you?
        ii) How long would you want them to be able to live off the money? This helps you determine how much life insurance to get.

2. **Is it important or a goal for you to leave money to your heirs?**
    a) Some people simply just want to leave a legacy of some kind to loved ones, even if beneficiaries don't "need" it. That is totally okay.
3. **Is your need for life insurance a temporary or permanent need?**
    a) A temporary need could be that of someone who has young children who can't care for themselves, or a partner who doesn't work. Maybe when your kids are grown, you may not have the same need for life insurance as you build up savings and assets.
    b) A permanent need could be wanting your loved ones to always be taken care of even if they're independent and in their own careers. You can also use permanent life insurance for wealth transfer strategies since money is generally tax-free to the beneficiary upon the insured's death. You can also use life insurance to help your heirs pay estate taxes or other financial obligations at your death.
4. **Are you worried about getting approved for coverage later in life?**
    a) The longer you wait to get permanent coverage, the more expensive premiums may get if you're not as healthy.
    b) Health screenings are usually required for permanent life approval.

5. **Are you looking for more tax-deferred growth?**
    a) Once you exhaust contributions to all your other tax-deferred accounts, a permanent life insurance policy could make sense to take advantage of more tax deferral and accessibility to funds while still providing a death benefit.
    b) Variable life policies have an investing component that may allow you to take advantage of the financial markets, while also providing a death benefit.

There are five main types of life insurance to know about.

1. **Term Life -** This is temporary life insurance that covers you for a specific amount of time (a "term"; e.g., 5–30 years). Term life will usually have lower premiums than permanent life insurance ("whole life"). After the term in the contract ends, the coverage ends. You may be able to purchase a "convertible term" policy which will act like a term policy but allow you the option to convert your term policy to a permanent policy with no health screening, which can be worth any extra premium if you think you'd like the option of permanent life insurance down the road.
2. **Whole Life -** Permanent policy that will not lapse as long as you pay the premiums, and the premiums stay the same throughout the life of the policy. This type of insurance builds up cash value that you can take loans from if needed and may possibly pay dividends depending on the company.
3. **Variable Whole Life -** Permanent life insurance with a fixed premium for the life of the policy. The difference

is, you can actually be invested in the stock or bond markets via mutual funds with a variable whole life policy, but this opens you up to market losses. So people with variable whole life policies generally need to have a higher tolerance for risk and understand what they're really buying. It's also important to understand the fees that will be associated with the mutual fund investments you choose in your account.

4. **Universal Life –** As previously discussed, with a whole life policy, you need to make the fixed premium payments every month on time to avoid lapse in coverage. Sometimes, life gets in the way and people may be unable to adhere to these structured payments. This is where a universal life policy can come in handy. Universal life gives you flexibility on the size of your premium payments and when you have to make them. This doesn't mean you want to go a long time without making payments, because the policy can essentially cannibalize itself by the insurance company deducting their regular fees, and the policy can run out of funds. But these policies do give some people peace of mind. They do tend to have higher fees but also usually pay interest.
5. **Variable Universal Life –** Variable universal life functions similarly to a variable whole life policy but gives you flexibility on your premium payments as well with the universal component. Again, when you see the term "variable," think of investing in the markets via mutual funds being offered by the insurance company and consider that you may want to have a higher risk tolerance for potential losses.

Annuities

Annuities are insurance contracts that allow you to pay a premium (either a large one-time payment or a series of payments) in exchange for a certain amount of income for your entire life that begins either at a certain age in the contract or immediately. They are usually purchased to help supplement or guarantee a certain amount of retirement income.

Sounds like a great deal, right? Guaranteed income if I give an insurance company some money? Well, not so fast.

Annuities can get complex, quickly. Some people may benefit greatly from this type of product, but others may not actually need it.

Annuities can be **fixed annuities** that credit your balance a fixed interest rate every year without any underlying investments to add the risk of loss of principal. Then they begin paying your monthly payments when they're needed or designated in the contract. Annuities may also be **variable annuities**, which allow you to invest in mutual funds in a similar way to a variable whole or universal life insurance policy. Remember, the term variable is usually associated with being able to invest the premiums into the stock or bond market.

Annuities don't come without fees and terms to look out for. They can carry mortality, administrative, and underlying investment fees depending on the type of annuity. They also carry penalties if you try to access the principal (your lump-sum value of your annuity) before age 59.5 in exchange for the IRS giving you the ability to have tax-deferred growth (either by interest rate credits to your account or profits from being invested in the markets being credited to your balance).

Wrapping It Up

There is a lot to learn about in the insurance world, but I hope you've found this to be a good primer and I've sparked some thought-provoking questions to help you make better decisions from here.

In the next few chapters, we move deeper into completing the financial puzzle with retirement planning.

This is really where the fun begins, and you start to see your vision for the future come alive. Onward!

Journal:

Take inventory of all of your insurance policies. List them below:

Policy Type (e.g., life, disability):	Coverage:	Deductible (if applies):

What type of policy could you add to help cover the risks that worry you most?

Part III

The Retirement Roadmap

Chapter 5
How to "Chill-tire"

Raise your hand if you want to retire eventually!

Odds are, your hand is up right now!

But do you really know what you will *want* or *need* in retirement? Do you need to know this now? These are some of the things we will get clear on in this chapter!

You'll Need Money, No Matter What ...

Just as we all have different personalities and genetics, we all have different desires for our retirement years. As many things you're learning in financial planning go, there is no one-size-fits-all retirement plan.

I know many people who are counting down the days until they've worked enough days and saved enough money so that they can go lie on a beach in Miami or escape to their mountain cabin that they've saved their whole lives for. I also know people who will never stop working and plan to run a business into their retirement age. Either direction you go, or somewhere in between, the key to planning a great retirement today is understanding what it is that YOU want, and not what society tells you a good retirement looks like.

I've helped you work though considering your definition of financial freedom. Now it's time to define your version of a great retirement.

I actually don't even like the word retirement anymore. I coined a new term for it all together: chill-tirement (pronounced chill-tire-ment).

Chilling out a bit more feels more attainable and, shall I say, flexible.

Many of you are probably thinking, *Nikki, I have no idea what I want in 20 or 30+ years.*

Or you know what you want, but not where. Maybe you know you want to be near your kids and grandkids, but not everyone knows where they'll be.

It's perfectly okay if you're unsure.

However, one thing is for certain: **you'll need money, no matter what.**

So it's good to start thinking about this now even with a fuzzy vision of what chill-tirement will hold for you. I see far too many people put this planning aside, because they feel like they don't have enough foresight into the future.

Your future self will thank you for the preparation work you put in today. Plus, people find their desires and passions later in life all the time, and by planning now, you'll be ready to design that life for yourself.

Also, thinking about one part of your life can sometimes help other parts come into focus.

Remember, money gives you flexibility. So don't let the unknown stop you from planning.

Your Perfect Average Day

I talk a lot with people in all stages of their lives about the "perfect average day."

Here is a good exercise to help you figure out what is most important to you, and in the next chapter we dive into some planning strategies to help get you there (yes, even if after this exercise, you're still shooting blanks on what your perfect average day is). These are actually questions a financial planner will likely be asking you in the financial planning process:

Your perfect average day in retirement exercise (no wrong answers, allow yourself to dream big!):

1. What is your ideal retirement age?
2. How much money would you like to live off every year in retirement (in today's dollars)? Think about if you want to live a luxurious lifestyle, simple lifestyle, or something in between?
3. Do you want to be mostly relaxing, doing charity work, pursuing an art or hobby, working in a business, or a combination of these?
4. Where do you see yourself living geographically? Would you have one home or multiple homes to take advantage of different seasons? Or maybe you want to travel extensively?
5. What tasks and activities would you be doing that bring you joy?
6. What are the tasks and activities that would NOT bring you joy? How could you outsource these?
7. What are your non-negotiables in retirement? Do you need to be near family? Or own a home in a specific

location? Have flexibility? Be able to take a specific number of vacations a year? Something else?

Did you allow yourself to dream a bit when answering these? You have to, because how else do you know what to work toward? The ultimate goal is maximizing happiness!

What if you were left with a bunch of blank answers because you just don't know? That's okay! Don't worry one bit because you are still going to plan for going down "a" road, you just aren't sure what is at the end of that road. Many people are in this boat, and it's actually not as much of a roadblock to retirement as you may think.

Saving with Intention

First off, I think it's important to understand something: many people call it "saving" for retirement. However, what most of us are actually doing is "investing" for retirement. We might be "saving" for retirement in a plain old savings account. However, when you're contributing to a specific type of retirement account like an IRA or a 401(k), your money is usually being invested in certain assets like stocks or bonds. Or you may be investing in real estate or something else. Don't worry, we will be reviewing investing in more detail in future chapters.

The terms "saving" and "investing" are often used interchangeably, although I do consider there to be a difference depending on whether you're truly just saving cash or you're invested in a specific market (but it's semantics for most people).

Here's the rub: far too many people are aimlessly contributing to retirement accounts like a 401(k), IRA, or even taxable brokerage accounts with no idea where it's actually going to get them in the end. (We will get into details on the best accounts to invest in for retirement in the next chapter.)

I was actually talking to a friend about this exact topic over wine one night (I sure do enjoy talking finance over a good vino). I asked her how much she had *hoped* to have for retirement based on her contributions to her 401(k). She said, "I don't know, I've never thought about it. I'm just contributing enough to get the match." She paused and said, "How about a million dollars?" I think she was just grabbing a number. However, turns out she would have had roughly $600,000 on her current contribution path, assuming an average return on her investment. I showed her some math that would get her to the million, and she said "Oh, wow, I can do that!" She was actually surprised and impressed with herself. That right there was enough for her to boost contributions a bit more to try to "become a millionaire!"

It's possible!

Most people don't take the time to figure out how much money their current investments are estimated to end up with in the end or what assets they're invested in within their retirement accounts, which we will discuss further in the investing chapters. Or they may not bump up contributions when they get a raise to improve their savings rate (as you make more money, your savings rate declines unless you save more of the money you make. Your savings rate is your money saved every month [or year] divided by your income for that period). Side note: I like including contributions to investment accounts in my savings rate calculations.

All of this is important to take time to analyze so that you know you're not aimlessly directing your money with no clue what the result will be.

Some people are only contributing what they can afford to, and that's fine, because you have to start somewhere. If this is you, don't feel discouraged at all. You're ahead of most people by a) contributing at all and b) reading this book to educate yourself. But, for people who have modest or significant cash flow that they're unsure what to do with, it certainly is important to have a plan of action so that every dollar works hard for you and helps you achieve your perfect average day in the end.

The Three Steps to Planning "Chill-tirement"

Good retirement planning starts with the "perfect average day" exercise we just went through at the start of this chapter to get an idea of how to structure your retirement plan. That is step 1. Think of that exercise as the blueprint. Then from the blueprint, we figure out what materials we need to actually "build" your retirement and how much money we will need for the end product.

Materials needed in the analogous context of our "blueprint" that helps us build the retirement plan, *could* be:

1. Different types of retirement accounts to optimize taxes now and in the future. (For example, you may get a tax deduction for contributions to certain types of retirement accounts. We will discuss the tax advantages of retirement accounts in the next chapter.)
2. Types of assets you're actually investing in within these accounts
3. Social Security
4. Pensions
5. Stock options

6. Medicare planning
7. Possibly using insurance contracts like annuities to help reduce the risk of running out of money or to fill an income gap

So that leads to step 2, which is figuring out "your chill-tirement number," taking into account inflation, that you need to have saved by retirement to live your perfect average day. Once you know what the lump-sum number is, you can then back into what you need to invest monthly or annually to get there based on a specific estimated investment return percentage. Knowing this number helps you avoid aimless contributions or spending. Maybe you won't buy the expensive Lexus SUV knowing that a couple of hundred dollars a month could better serve your retirement account rather than going to a car payment, right?

There are many retirement calculators available on the internet that you can plug numbers into to figure out "your chill-tirement number." This is actually an exercise I walk people through in my training program, but here are some examples of how you could use an online retirement calculator to figure out "your number" and how much you should be putting aside regularly.

Some popular retirement calculators online include

- https://www.nerdwallet.com/investing/retirement-calculator
- https://www.bankrate.com/retirement/retirement-plan-calculator/

It may help to pull one of these up online as you continue reading this chapter.

Once you determine your number, you need to invest to get there. There are a number of factors that you have to consider first: your contributions, your rate of return, and inflation rates.

Your deposits/contributions to the retirement account(s)

This is how much you're contributing either monthly or yearly, depending on the calculator settings.

Your estimated rate of return expected

Your rate of return is the percentage that your account is expected to grow every year (annualized to average out the ups and downs over time). Now, this return you choose shouldn't come out of thin air. It will depend on what your money is invested in, which will lead you to what your estimated expected return should be. We will be diving into details in the investing chapters of this book, but, generally speaking, equities (aka stocks) have higher returns than bonds (which pay you interest over a specific period of time). For example, for the past 100 years, the S&P 500, which is the most inclusive stock index representing our stock market, has returned roughly 10% annually with dividends reinvested. Bonds, however, have historically lower annualized returns due to the nature of the lower risk profile.

Here is a visual from Vanguard showing historical returns of a portfolio based on whether it's invested more in stocks or bonds. The first image shows a portfolio invested heavier into bonds at 80% and stocks at only 20%. The historical annual return of that portfolio is 7.5%. The second portfolio is heavier into stocks at 80% with bonds at 20%. This portfolio has a historical annual return of 11.1%. That's a 3.6% difference in return between these two portfolios. Doesn't sound like much, right?

20% stocks / 80% bonds

Historical Risk/Return (1926-2021)

Average annual return: **7.5%**
Best year (1982): **40.7%**
Worst year (1931): **-10.1%**
Years with a loss: **16 of 96**

Source: https://investor.vanguard.com/investor-resources-education/education/model-portfolio-allocation

80% stocks / 20% bonds

Historical Risk/Return (1926-2021)

Average annual return: **11.1%**
Best year (1933): **45.4%**
Worst year (1931): **-34.9%**
Years with a loss: **24 of 96**

Source: https://investor.vanguard.com/investor-resources-education/education/model-portfolio-allocation

Now, here is the difference between dollar returns of a portfolio with a 3.6% interest rate variant (3.6% difference between each interest rate). So the middle line is an 11.1% return, the red line is a 7.5% return, and the bottom line is a 3.9% return. This is for the purpose of proving the point that using the proper interest rate based on your portfolio allocation is important:

This is a compound interest example with a $10,000 initial investment with $500 a month contributed for 30 years at three different rates of return (3.9%, 7.5%, 11.1%).

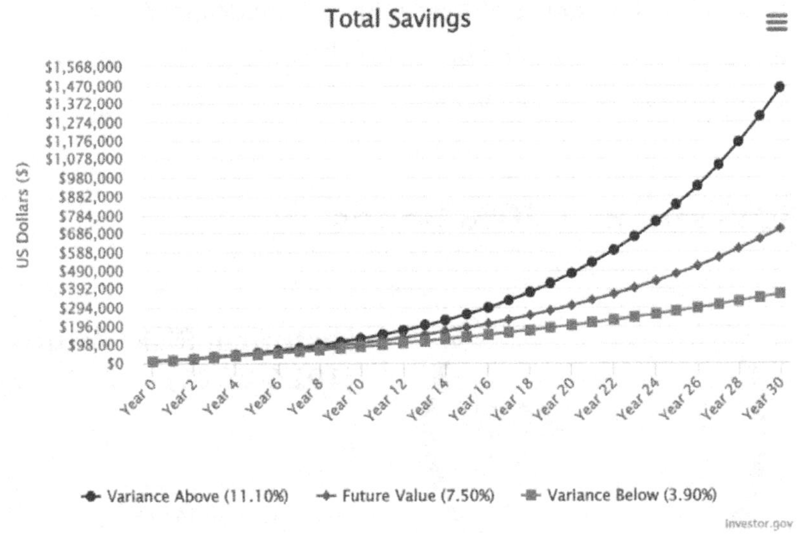

See how much a 3.6% return difference makes in terms of how much money you end up with in the end? The return compounding at 11.1% earns you $744,498 more than a return compounding at 7.5%. That's a lot of cash, my friend!

Expected inflation rates

This is the real kicker ... inflation is the increase in the cost of goods over time, and it's real. So, when we do retirement planning, we have to estimate what we think inflation will be over time. Why? Have you tried to fill up your grocery cart with $100 lately? It surely doesn't buy what it used to! So, our goal with investing for retirement is to make sure our money grows at a higher rate than inflation over time, so that we can buy just as many goods with our dollars later.

The image below is what inflation rates have looked like going back to the 1960s. The Federal Reserve (aka the Fed) is the entity that conducts monetary policy in the United States. Their goal is to target inflation of 2% per year, ideally. They don't want to see inflation too low, or too high. They have levers to pull, for example, tightening or loosening the money supply to discourage or encourage banks to lend money to consumers. If inflation occurs at the Fed's target rate, that means your dollars buy 2% less every year (which you can see below that sometimes it is, and sometimes it isn't, but on average inflation has hung around the 2% range since the 1990s).

The translation of all of this: If inflation is 2% over time, you want to earn at least 2% return in your portfolio to break even on your purchasing power. You need to earn more than 2% if you want your purchasing power to actually be growing!

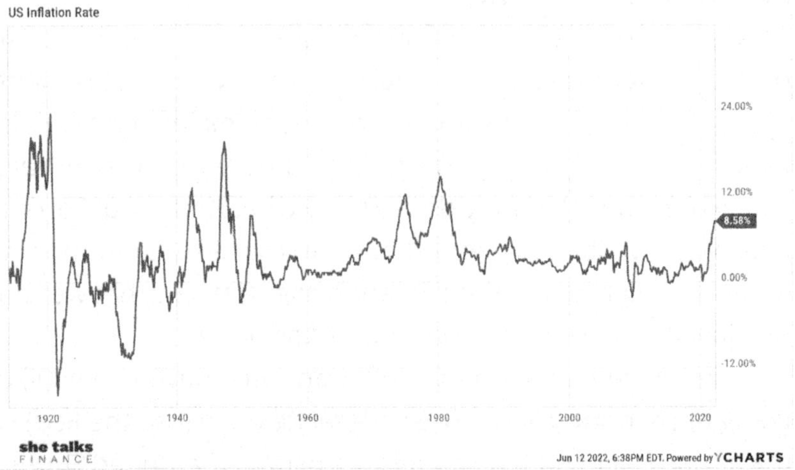

So, you will want to be sure to plug in an expected inflation rate into your retirement calculator to account for this phenomenon.

Step 3 is going to be choosing the right retirement accounts to make your deposits to. We get more into detail on this topic in the next chapter.

Generally, you're trying not only to manage reaching your monetary goal for retirement, but also to manage taxes now and later! It's a delicate dance, and this is where choosing the right types of accounts is vital.

Here are the main three types of accounts:

1. **Tax-deferred:** These types of accounts will defer any taxes on monetary gains in your account until later in retirement. You don't avoid taxation; you just defer it. People who have high income today and expect their income and tax rates to be lower later in life tend to choose these accounts.

2. **Tax-advantaged:** These types of accounts will usually offer a tax-free benefit on monetary gains later in retirement in exchange for you paying taxes today on any contributions.
3. **Taxable:** There is no tax deferment or advantage; you simply pay taxes on any capital gains, dividends, or interest as you incur them (if you buy $1,000 worth of stock and sell it a year later for $2,000, you have a $1,000 capital gain that you will have to pay taxes on for that tax year that you sold). You can also write off losses in these accounts as you receive them (within limits).

Time to Get to the Good Stuff

So, now you have an idea of what retirement planning entails and how to think about the future (or you understand how not to let it be a roadblock if you don't know what you want).

It's time to really get into the good stuff going forward from here. The next chapter will review how to choose the right retirement accounts for your goals and tax situation; then the following chapters will get into the vehicle that really gets us there: investing strategies.

Journal:

Go play around with a retirement calculator online. What is it saying you need to save every month, or year, to reach your goals?

Chapter 6
Guide to the Best Retirement Account for You

Disclaimer: The strategies and accounts discussed are for educational purposes. There may be nuances to the rules that can't be elaborated on in a book. Always consult a tax or finance professional on your individual situation.

In the last chapter we went over how to draft out your "blueprint to retirement" and figure out what you want to work toward (and if you don't yet know what you want to work toward, you learned how you're still going to start building anyway since you know at a minimum you'll need money!).

In this chapter, I'll help you get familiar with the accounts and other options that actually help you take the action toward building your retirement (or, as I like to call it, "chill-tirement") nest egg.

The "Materials" You Need to Build Your Retirement

As you know, it's all about the money. You have to find a healthy balance of how you can live a good life today, while still putting away enough money to live a good life later. Knowing your "chill-tirement number" that you'll need in retirement is what helps you figure this out. You went through this in the previous chapter learning how to work with a retirement calculator. Once you know how much to put away monthly or yearly to get you there, you can start living a bit more in the now with the rest of the money you may have (take that vacation or buy that boat).

Once you know your chill-tirement number, it's time to get familiar with the types of accounts that are available to you and how to decide which account (or combination of accounts) will be best for you. You also will want to consider any other "materials" that may be available to you, like stock options, Health Savings Accounts, and more.

Which retirement account should you choose?

There are a few main types of accounts that you can use to save and invest for retirement. The following sections will give you a comprehensive list, broken down into three sections: accounts that apply if you are employed by someone else, individual retirement accounts not associated with an employer or your own business, and accounts that apply if you are self-employed.

Retirement Accounts If You're Employed by Someone Else (Not Self-employed)

1. **Traditional 401(k)**

A Traditional 401(k) is a retirement plan that your employer sets up and gives you the ability to contribute to. Your employer may also match your contributions (up to certain amounts). An employer match alone is a great reason to contribute to your employer's 401(k) because it's FREE MONEY. Free money is the best kind of money.

Keep in mind that your employer may have a vesting schedule that requires you to stay with the company for a certain amount of time to be able to keep the full value of the matched contributions from them.

Contributions get invested into the markets (usually stocks and bonds) based on your risk tolerance. Risk tolerance is how comfortable you are losing money, and investment managers usually will ask you a few questions to figure out if you have a conservative, moderate, or aggressive risk tolerance.

You get a tax deduction for contributing to a Traditional 401(k) as well. You'll learn more about this in my chapters on taxes, but the money you defer from your paycheck into this account is an "above the line" tax deduction to lower your adjusted gross income up to certain limits ($23,000 as of this writing—please check IRS.gov for updated limits). This is good, and it helps you lower your overall federal tax liability!

2. **Roth 401(k)**

A Roth 401(k) acts similar to a Traditional 401(k); however, the major difference is, you do NOT get any tax deductions for deferring money from your paycheck into this account.

Any account that is classified as a Roth is allowing you to pay taxes today on contributions in order to be able to take out the growth in the account tax-free, later in retirement. Those who pay low tax rates now tend to utilize Roth more to lock in today's low rate, especially if they think tax rates will be much higher when they retire.

Your employer may still do a contribution match if you contribute here, but the matches will go into a Traditional

401(k) account for you (recent Secure 2.0 law now allows employers the option to directly match into Roth accounts).

When making the decision to choose contributing to a Traditional or Roth 401(k), remember that in retirement the idea is you have less income, leading to lower tax rates anyway, which may lead people to choose Traditional. However, there are a lot of unknowns to say for sure what taxes will look like later for you!

The main considerations should be: 1) Are you in an attractive tax rate now that you'd like to lock in by using a Roth 401(k)? 2) Do you think taxes will be higher or lower in the future for your expected income in retirement? 3) Do you need a tax deduction today or not? (If not, Roth is an option for you.)

3. **SIMPLE IRA**

The SIMPLE IRA may be offered to you by your employer. It functions similarly to a 401(k); however, the max contribution limits are lower ($16,000 as of this writing—please check IRS.gov for updated limits).

4. **403(b)**

A 403(b) account functions like a Traditional 401(k), with similar contribution limits and tax deductibility of those contributions. 403(b)s are offered to employees of public schools and certain 501(c)(3) tax-exempt organizations.

The key difference from a 401(k) is that a 403(b) can only be invested in mutual funds or annuities, which can tend to have pretty high fees depending on the offerings.

Many teachers have been prey to some pretty shady practices by insurance salespeople with these plans. I suggest you educate yourself on how to tell what the investment options are and the fees associated with them. I do a lot of education around this in my training to empower people to be able to confidently see through some of these sales practices.

If you're young and someone is trying to sell you a variable annuity, that is your key to asking a lot of questions. Half of the time, however, there is not enough education around the products being offered by the plan administrators, but we've seen improvements here and there.

5. **457 Deferred Compensation Plan**

There are two main types of deferred compensation plans. One is a governmental 457(b), and the other is a non-governmental 457(b). There are slight differences between the two.

The governmental 457(b) has employee funds held in trust and protected on their behalf. Non-governmental plans need to be unfunded, and the funds contributed must be subject to the employer's creditors in the event of bankruptcy or litigation. Non-governmental 457(b) plans may also be referred to as "top hat" plans for highly compensated employees.

Most people who work for state or local governments will have access to a governmental 457(b) deferred compensation plan. In an eligible 457(b) plan, you're able to contribute up to a certain limit from your salary every year ($23,000 as of this writing—see IRS.gov for updated limits). There are also special catch-up provisions three years prior to retirement that allow you to contribute even higher amounts.

A 457 plan, whether it's governmental or non-governmental, also allows you to get access to the funds earlier than age 59.5 if you separate from service before then. These plans are also not subject to the 10% early withdrawal penalty. The

457 is another great way to take advantage of tax-deferred retirement investing; however, just like the 403(b) plan, check your investment options and fees to optimize your returns.

6. **Pension Plans**

If you're lucky enough to be offered a pension, that's awesome! Some employers are still offering pension plans which involve the employer primarily making contributions to your pension. You may have a plan that allows for you to contribute to it as well. There is likely to be a vesting schedule that requires you to stay with the company for a certain amount of time to be able to receive your pension later. Check with your employer to find this information out so that you can make the best decisions if you're considering leaving your job that does offer a pension.

Individual Retirement Accounts (Not Associated with an Employer or Your Own Business)

You can open a "personal" IRA (individual retirement account) in addition to any other retirement accounts as long as you have earned income (earned wages from working either as an employee or from running or owning a business). I call it a personal IRA because it's not sponsored by your employer, or your business if you're self-employed.

IRAs are used by individuals to take advantage of tax deferral or tax advantages that you can't get in a non-retirement account.

There are some limitations to either contributing or deducting your contribution on your taxes based on:

1. Which IRA you're contributing to
2. Your income
3. Your accessibility to other retirement plans

Don't get overwhelmed, though. I will cover how to navigate this in the descriptions below, and most people are not affected.

There are two types of personal IRAs. Here are descriptions of each and details of how to navigate their limitations.

1. **Traditional IRA**

A Traditional IRA is a plain and simple tax-deferred retirement account that allows you to potentially get a tax deduction for contributing to it. Here are the steps to understanding how taxation works on contributions and growth in the account.

TRADITIONAL IRA TAXATION

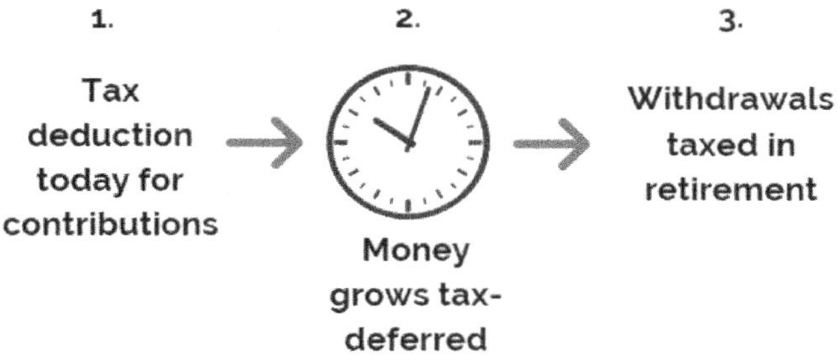

Here are the caveats to watch out for with the Traditional IRA:

If you make too much income AND you have access to a retirement plan at work, you can still contribute to this account, but you may not be able to fully DEDUCT the contributions from your taxes. *(If you're self-employed with a SEP-IRA or Solo-401(k), this counts as access to an employer plan because your business sponsors it.)*

Tip: If you find out that you make too much to deduct your Traditional IRA contribution, you may want to see if you're eligible to contribute to a Roth IRA at that point for the tax advantages in retirement since you're having to pay taxes on the contributions anyway.

2. **Roth IRA**

When you hear the word Roth in front of anything [Roth IRA, or Roth 401(k)], think, pay taxes now on contributions in order to have the benefit of taking the money and growth out of retirement tax-free. It's pretty awesome, but it's not necessarily a no-brainer, and not everyone can contribute to one.

The Roth makes a lot of sense for people paying lower tax rates today. So you're essentially locking in your current tax rate, and your money gets to grow and grow, then in retirement if tax rates are higher than when you made the contribution, you won the tax game!

It can also go the other way though. It gets riskier for people in higher tax brackets who choose Roth. You can lose the tax game too, and potentially have given up a tax deduction that you may have had by opting for a Traditional IRA instead if tax rates are actually lower in retirement.

This is why I love "tax diversification" by using both the Traditional in high income years and the Roth in lower income years if you can. None of us have a crystal ball to know what our economy and tax rates will look like later, so you reduce your risk a bit by having money in both pots.

ROTH IRA TAXATION

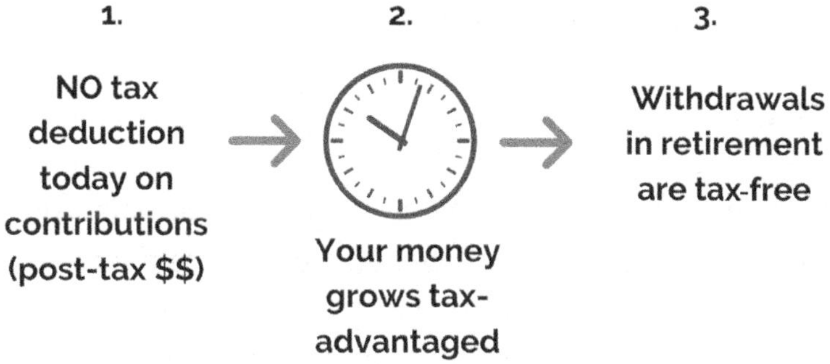

Here is the caveat to watch out for with the Roth IRA:

- If you have too much income, you may not be able to contribute to a Roth IRA at all. (*Side note: if you have a Roth 401(k), there are no income limits, which is great.*)

I suggest keeping up with the IRS.gov website to stay up to date on the contribution limit (currently $7,000 a year max as of this writing), income, and deductibility limits for these accounts!

Retirement Account Options If You're Self-Employed

(Note: I will be discussing these plans in the context of being a business owner with no W-2 employees except for yourself or a

spouse. If you do have W-2 employees, you can still set up any of the main employer-sponsored plans outlined in the first section, and you'll have to make contributions on behalf of all eligible employees):

Remember, you can have one of these self-employed retirement plans in addition to a personal IRA. You may have multiple active plans from this list, but you would only be able to contribute to one type of plan during a calendar year for tax purposes.

1. **SEP-IRA**

This is a great account for self-employed individuals who are looking to get more money invested into a retirement account than the personal IRA allows you to do. It's typically the first plan a business owner will open up. The contribution is going to be a certain percentage of your business net income up to a certain limit ($69,000 as of this writing—see IRS.gov for updated limits). Remember, if you contribute to a SEP-IRA, you can also contribute to a personal IRA; however, you may be subject to income limitations that determine how much, if any, of a Traditional IRA specifically would be deductible.

2. **Solo-401(k)**

If you're liking how the SEP-IRA sounds but you'd like to get even more money into retirement, a Solo-401(k) may be a good match. This allows you to contribute as the employee of your business and the employer. So, you are able to defer up to a certain amount of your salary (if you have a W-2) or business income (if you file schedule C) as the employee ($23,000 as of this writing—see IRS.gov for updated limits), and 25% of your salary or business income as the employer. That extra salary deferral as the employee is what helps you increase contributions potentially above the SEP-IRA limits. Keep in mind, different people have their businesses taxed in different ways, so this will affect the calculations here. I will talk more in detail about this in the tax chapter, and I teach how to plan retirement contributions in more detail in my online training program.

3. **SIMPLE IRA**

The SIMPLE IRA is essentially a Traditional IRA with higher limits ($16,000 as of this writing—see IRS.gov for updated limits). These are very simple, low-cost plans to set up; however, the contribution limits tend to be less than what you can get with a SEP-IRA or Solo-401(k), so it's usually less likely that someone would set up a SIMPLE IRA over the former two options.

4. **Pension Plan**

We discussed the pension plan in the previous section, but something you may not know is that if you're self-employed and a high-income earner, you are able to create a pension plan for your business. This works best if you're working alone or with a spouse, as you'll need to contribute to all W-2 employees or partners if you go this route (which may be fine, just something to be aware of). This is a more advanced strategy for when you start maxing out contributions to other self-employed options like a Solo-401(k) or SEP-IRA. This can be a powerful strategy if you're in higher tax brackets, because the employer contributions can be massive (multiple six-figures), which is considered a tax deduction from your business income, which in turn is lowering your taxable income significantly. You will still need to invest these funds suitably and make sure you work with the right plan administrator to set this up properly.

Using Other Retirement Tools Outside of Retirement Accounts to Reach Your Goals

It's really easy to think only about the retirement accounts that I have outlined in this chapter for reaching goals, and these are going to be important core accounts to have. However, there are other materials that may be accessible to you that can help make your retirement great and supplement what you have invested in other places.

Roth conversions

In a Roth conversion, you take Traditional IRA or 401(k) money, and you decide to convert it to a Roth. This triggers you to take whatever amount of money you're converting, and it gets added to your income on your tax return to pay tax on it. Remember, there is no tax deduction for Roth contributions! However, those who are in favorable tax brackets, or made less income one year, may find a Roth conversion to be a wise choice. We will touch more on this in the tax chapter.

Stock compensation

Corporations have been leaning on different forms of stock compensation to reward and retain their executives and employees for years. If you work for a corporation that offers stock-based compensation, it can be a great way to acquire more money for retirement or other goals.

The main types of stock compensation are:

1. **Non-qualified (NQSO) and incentive stock options (ISO):** Stock options give you the right, but not the obligation to purchase stock at a certain price in the future. These options usually come with a vesting schedule that dictates when you can actually take action to buy the stock shares at the specified price (aka strike or exercise price). Stock options don't come without risk though, as there is always risk in company stock of the stock price declining lower than when you bought the shares. However, they can also be great ways to accumulate wealth over the long run, especially if you're working for a successful company. One thing to watch out for with stock options is too much concentration of your wealth in your own company stock. You may want to work with a professional to diversify out into other assets as your wealth grows. The taxation of stock options can get complex as well, so working with a tax professional is advised if you receive or exercise your options.
2. **Restricted stock:** Restricted stock is granted to key employees and generally holds value for the employee no matter if the stock goes up or down. When a company grants restricted stock, it usually comes with a vesting schedule to actually receive the stock. There is tax due on the value of the stock granted at vesting. There is also a feature called the 83(b) election, which allows someone to pay taxes on the value of the stock

when it's granted before it vests with the goal that the stock will appreciate much higher at vesting (helping to avoid a larger tax bill). This isn't always a no-brainer decision, but it's good to be aware of the 83(b) election, because it has to be made within 30 days of when the restricted shares are granted.

3. **Restricted stock units:** Restricted stock units are similar to restricted stock; however, they aren't eligible for the 83(b) election. You pay taxes on the value of the stock at your vesting date.

You may have available to you an employee stock purchase plan (ESPP) at work as well that allows you to get a discount on company stock that you can purchase.

Annuities: The bad ... and the good

Annuities are insurance contracts that allow you to pay a premium to the insurance company in return for a guaranteed stream of income payments in the future. Many people use annuities to supplement part of their retirement income if they're worried about running out of money. Annuities have received a bad reputation for being oversold to individuals who didn't really need them to line a salesperson's pockets with commissions, but there could be cases where they're right for some people.

There are many types of annuities, and I covered these in the insurance chapter, but I will cover the main two here:

1. **Variable annuities:** These are annuities that allow you to actually invest your premiums into the financial market via mutual funds. Most people don't buy variable annuities until they have maxed out tax-deferred

savings elsewhere via retirement plans outlined in the beginning of this chapter. The idea is that your money will grow, and you'll be able to get a larger guaranteed stream of income in retirement. They can also come with riders on the policies that allow you to have a guaranteed amount that you'll be able to pull from the policy later. Variable annuities can come with very high yearly mortality and administrative fees, and in addition to this, the mutual funds you're being invested in also can carry fees upwards of 1%+ of your assets every year. It can also be quite expensive to get out of these contracts without losing a hefty chunk of your capital, so you want to make sure it's the right move for you.

2. **Straight life annuity:** This is the preferred route for many people if they're concerned about not having enough money throughout their entire retirement. You pay a lump sum of money to the insurance company for the annuity in return for guaranteed monthly payments for the rest of your life. Think of this type of annuity as one you'd buy later in life, closer to when you'd actually need it. If you have a long life, you may get payments back in excess of what you paid the insurance company. It's also possible that you may have a shorter life than expected and not fully benefit from the annuity.

A helpful tip when it comes to choosing if an annuity is right for you is to consider your age. Due to the high fees on many annuities (particularly variable or indexed annuities that track the stock market), it usually makes more sense for young people to be directly invested in the markets instead of via a high-fee insurance contract. Most people invest in the market and grow their nest egg, and once they have an idea of what that will yield them in income later, they can consider a straight life annuity via a lump-sum payment with their invested funds.

Medicare and Social Security Insurance

The Federal Insurance Contributions Act (FICA) is a United States federal payroll contribution to fund Social Security and Medicare for individuals. You have to work and earn a certain amount of money that you pay FICA taxes on to acquire enough credits to be eligible for benefits in your lifetime. Not every job will require you to pay FICA tax, such as some state and local government positions.

Social Security pays you a certain amount of money for the rest of your life as of a certain retirement age. Many people are forced to live off Social Security alone in retirement as they don't have any other retirement savings. I like to think of Social Security as a bonus, not a source of income to fully rely on if possible, because it's simply not enough money for most people. However, it can be a great supplement and worth earning enough credits from working to qualify.

Medicare is a federal health insurance program for those age 65 or older. It's not free—you pay taxes to fund the program (part of FICA tax paid), and you pay Medicare premiums for the coverage (just like regular health insurance) when you finally do qualify at 65. Medicare doesn't cover everything, especially extended long-term care stays (which can get expensive). So it can be wise to continue to save and invest with healthcare needs in mind while you're young or utilize something called a Health Savings Account if you qualify.

Between both Social Security and Medicare, they help you manage retirement by supplementing your income and giving you health coverage that is affordable.

Choosing the Right Accounts

You may be thinking to yourself, *Wow, there is more to this than I thought and a lot of accounts to choose from*, and you may have access to many of these. You're right ... so I created this graphic to help you figure out what accounts and tools you should be considering first, before you move to anything else.

Hierarchy of Where to Allocate Cash

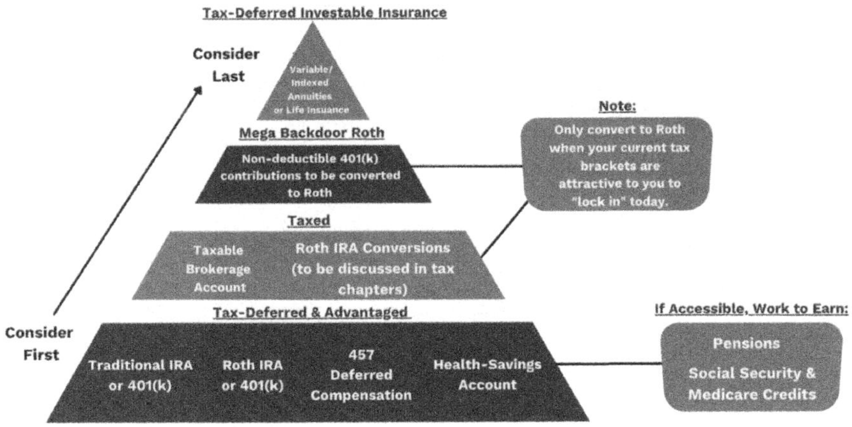

In the next chapter, we get into everyone's favorite topic (including mine) ... how to invest!

But you can't do the investing without knowing what type of retirement accounts you're investing in. So I hope this chapter has given you the foundation you need to make that decision going forward, and now it's time to learn how to collect some dividends and truly "compound your money."

Journal:

Take inventory of all of your retirement accounts. If you're unsure of the type of account (e.g., 401(k), Roth IRA, taxable), contact your account provider and they can help. List them below:

Account:	Type:	Balance:

Part IV

Investing Like A Pro

Chapter 7
The Wealth Multiplier

In the last few chapters, we talked about how to get more clarity on what you really want so that you can make a better plan going forward. We also touched on the fact that even if you can't figure out your desires, it's still important to work toward growing your nest egg and at least have flexibility.

No matter what you decide to do, you know you'll need money!

So now we dive into my favorite topic: investing! This is how you actually grow your money.

Your Retirement Plan Is the Blueprint, but Investing Is What Actually Gets You to the Finished Product

Wealth is mostly built through investing in different assets. Can you "save" yourself to wealth? Sure ... if you have a huge money windfall or a high revenue generating business. However, most people need to invest if they want their money to compound and grow over time. Even if you "save your way to wealth," your money will still lose purchasing power over time to inflation if you don't invest it in some way. Remember, inflation is the rising cost of goods over time. This is why $100 at the grocery store gets you diddly-squat these days.

Your retirement plan (more specifically, knowing your "chill-tirement number" to help you reach your lifestyle goals), along with your risk tolerance, is the blueprint for how much and how you should be investing.

Investing is a topic that goes wide and deep, but in this chapter I plan to walk you through how an investment strategy can align with your definition of financial freedom, why investing is so important, and the basics of how to actually get invested.

The following chapter will get more into the technicalities of investment strategies and how to actually construct a portfolio.

Why Investing Is So Important

We learned in earlier chapters about inflation (the increasing cost of goods and services) and how, over time, this eats away at how much "stuff" your money can buy. This is why we invest: to make returns that either keep up with or outpace the rate of inflation.

If inflation averages 3% in a year, we want our investment returns to be at least 3% or higher on average to keep up with it. However, this is much easier said than done, depending on where the economy is at times. Sometimes we have a healthy economy, so savers earn more interest on their money and inflation may be low. Sometimes, the economy isn't very healthy at all (remember the 2008 financial crisis?).

I know far too many people who don't start investing until later in life, even though they actually could have started earlier. It's usually happening because of lack of understanding of the markets and asset classes or fear of losing the money they have. But no one gets very wealthy without investing in some shape or form. You're in the right place though, so give yourself a pat on the back for me.

If you're in a fearful mindset around investing, keep in mind that there are conservative ways to invest without taking on a lot of risk! It's not one-size-fits-all, and you can invest in so many different ways. So don't let this deter you. The other thing that I find that helps is simply educating yourself about the markets and how they've acted historically. Look at all the ups and downs and see for yourself how a long-term investment strategy did.

Take a look at this chart of the S&P 500, which represents the 500 largest U.S. companies (keep in mind these companies change throughout the years as our economy changes).

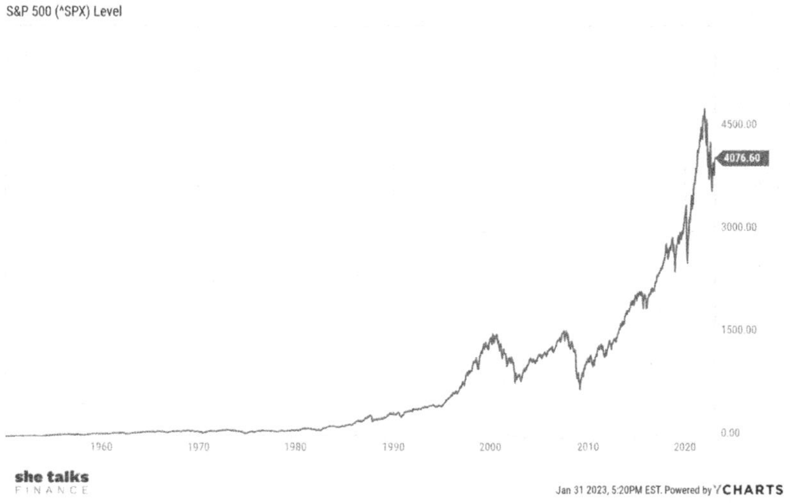

Source: YCharts.com

Being invested in an S&P 500 fund is also known as being invested in the "stock market," and you can see that there were many times that the price went down over the years, but, overall, we continued to see the index march higher ... and higher ... and higher. So, a buy-and-hold long-term investment strategy has paid investors handsomely.

Now, past performance doesn't mean future performance will look like this, but we have the data that shows this has worked, and until we see a major shift in either our economy or how our government handles policy, we're expecting innovation to push us (and our stocks) forward.

Why Understanding Investing Is Important Even If You Have Someone Doing It for You

As you've learned so far, without investing, it's really hard for most people to reach long-term financial goals. So this is obviously an important topic. You may be thinking, however, *I don't need to know much because I have a 401(k) at work which takes care of it*, or *This is why I hired a financial advisor to help me; I don't have time to learn.*

Well, I am here to tell you that even if those things are true, it's still important to have a baseline of knowledge to help you navigate things that eat into your returns over time. These can be things like funds with high fees offered by some employer retirement plans and advisors, costly or overly complex investment strategies being used, or even unnecessary expensive life insurance or annuities being masked as a sound "retirement plan" (403(b)s and 457 deferred compensation plans offered to teachers or those working for governments are often especially terrible with this).

It also helps you have a more fulfilling relationship with anyone you work with. You'll also be able to vet any new advisors you're looking to work with more confidently with questions.

Can I Invest on My Own?

The real question that I get often is, "Is it possible to be a do-it-yourself investor to save money on fees that an advisor charges?"

Yes, absolutely.

Investing doesn't have to be difficult, and the fund world has honestly made it cheaper and easier than ever with a very low barrier of knowledge there (I cover investing in funds in the next chapter). I have created training programs that actually teach people the ins and outs of the market so that they can make their own investing decisions thoughtfully or better understand the investments they're in via someone else's guidance. So I am all about the do-it-yourself investor, and I have been one myself for over a decade.

Investing wisely is not rocket science, contrary to what the finance industry has led people to believe. It's extremely learnable, and a little effort here can go a long way!

You'd be surprised to know that I have talked to many people who had money going into their 401(k)s at work, having no idea what was actually happening. I was having a conversation with a friend over lunch about the stock market, and she said, "Oh, I'd never invest in the stock market; it's way too risky for me." I asked her if she had a 401(k) at work, and she replied, "Yes, I have money going to it from every paycheck."

I replied, "Well, then you're highly likely invested in the stock market in some capacity." She was surprised, and when we looked at her statements together, sure enough, she was invested in a version of an S&P 500 index fund. That's being invested in the stock market, all right!

I have had this same conversation a multitude of times as well. No one is taught this stuff in school, so there is truly no way for people to know unless they research it. All we're told is to put money into your retirement account, but not how it's actually invested, or that it's invested at all.

With an employer-sponsored 401(k) or other type of plan, they have someone administering the plan and managing your investments for you. But a great travesty that exists for those who contribute to individual IRAs or self-employed retirement plans is not realizing that after you contribute the money, you usually have to actually get it invested yourself unless you hire someone to do it for you.

There are many contributions likely sitting in cash, not in the markets earning compounding interest or market returns at all, because the holders had no idea that it worked that way.

This is even more reason to get a feel for the basics of investing: so that you can avoid big mistakes! We will cover the how-tos as you read through this and the next chapter.

Investing for Your Definition of Financial Freedom and Lifestyle

Everyone has a different definition of financial freedom and a different desired lifestyle, and you can invest in a way that fits you. Don't assume that any one investment is "a must do" because someone else said so.

Think of it this way: investing in hard real estate (the actual homes, not shares of Real Estate Investment Trusts) requires a lot of work and money to be able to manage the investment.

Real Estate Investment Trusts (REITs) will be covered in detail in the next chapter.

You may have to hire contractors to renovate, keep up with maintenance, spend money on repairs, and manage the property to collect rent. You can hire people to help you manage your real estate, but, of course, that needs to be factored into your returns. Maybe your lifestyle doesn't fit that, and you have no desire to do any of this (maybe you want to be a nomad and backpack around the world like me).

Maybe buying and holding land in up-and-coming areas is more fitting for you versus actual houses.

Or maybe the idea of being a real estate investor excites you, and you have a knack for renovations and negotiating real estate deals. You may find a clever way to house-hack by buying a duplex, living in it, and renting out a unit. Maybe you want to make money renting a home out on Airbnb.

I know for myself, so far, I have had an extremely nomadic life. My husband and I are constantly traveling and moving. For that reason, we've actually been renters of our primary residence! It has been cheaper for us to rent versus buy in the areas we wanted to live. So we took the savings from renting and invested it in the markets. This strategy has served us well.

Although my husband and I have tried renovating a property to flip, it was not fun for us, and we lost money. We prefer paper assets like stocks, for example. I get my real estate exposure through shares of REITs (this gets me commercial real estate exposure that I otherwise wouldn't be able to obtain easily). We also hold physical gold, but this doesn't take much work! Land in up-and-coming areas is something that also excites us as a physical asset (with the potential to build on it down the road). So we invest in a way that fits our lifestyle and desires, and I encourage people to do the same.

The Right Investing Strategy Starts with Risk Tolerance

Risk tolerance and risk capacity are the first step to any kind of investing. What good is your investing strategy if you can't even hold through the tough times due to emotions or investing more than you can afford to? The idea is to get invested and STAY invested to grow wealth long-term!

Risk tolerance is how much risk (also known as: the possibility of losing money) you're comfortably able to take on and sleep well at night. People fall on a spectrum from conservative through moderate to aggressive risk tolerance. Conservative risk-takers do not like the feeling of losing money and tend to be invested in lower risk assets that generate lower returns naturally. Aggressive risk-takers usually don't mind the idea of losing money if it means higher return potential.

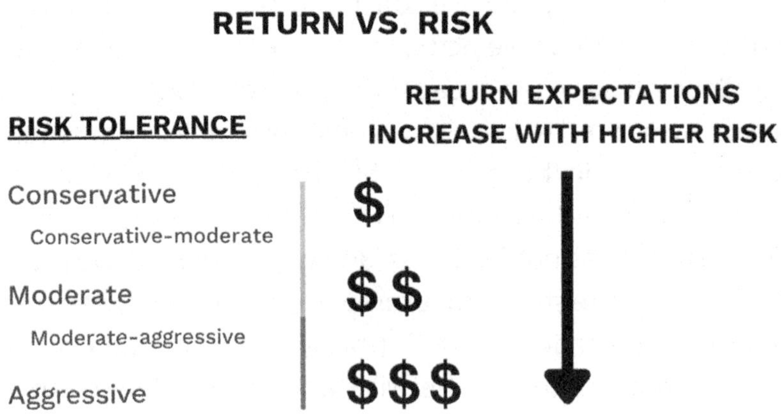

Source: She Talks Finance Training Program

Risk capacity is a bit different. This is your ABILITY to actually afford to lose money. Sure, you may be an aggressive risk-taker, but if you have low risk capacity due to the fact that you're in a lot of debt and have no savings, you don't really have the ability to lose more money with no consequences. Another example of someone with low risk capacity is a retiree who really depends on the money they have left to survive for the rest of their life. This retiree doesn't have the capacity to take on big risks at that stage of their life.

But let's say you generally have your financial house in order. You have savings, you have sufficient income to pay the bills plus extra, and you're young with many working years left and no children. You have higher risk capacity than do the people in the prior examples. You have many years to work and make money you've lost back. You also have extra income that you can invest without compromising getting your bills paid.

Again, if you can't stay in the investing game, what good is it? The goal is to be properly investing for your risk tolerance AND risk capacity so you can survive the downturns and not panic out of the market.

The goal is reaching your financial goals AND getting a good night's sleep!

How to Actually Invest

Someone who wants to get invested has quite a few options ranging from very hands-on to very hands-off!

The first step is deciding one of among three ways to invest (or a combination of a few or all of these):

1. Do it yourself with your own brokerage account.
2. Hire a financial advisor to do it for you.

3. Use a robo-advisor (which is a brokerage that offers automated investing).

DIY investor

Doing it yourself would require you to simply open a brokerage account at any of the major firms out there today. Some of the top brokerage firms for U.S. citizens are Fidelity, Charles Schwab, TD Ameritrade, E-Trade, Vanguard, and Interactive Brokers. From there, you can buy and sell assets (securities like stocks or bonds) as you wish. You would simply deposit money from a checking or savings account, and once it hits your brokerage account, you can invest it as you please.

Don't worry, we will cover the different types of assets in detail in the next chapter.

Hire an advisor

If you really don't feel comfortable investing your own money, or you don't have the time to handle it (which many people don't), then the right move is to get help! I do suggest hiring an independent, fee-only, fiduciary financial advisor. Even better, hire a CERTIFIED FINANCIAL PLANNER™ professional (this is a designation in the financial industry that is very respected). You can find an independent advisor who is registered in your state on https://www.xyplanningnetwork.com/

Robo-advisor

Many people have gone robo over the years! Robo-advisors ask you a series of questions to determine your risk tolerance and goals, and they automatically invest for you. The downside is that this strategy may not invest you in all of the assets that you want to be in. Some robo-advisors tend to focus on stocks and bonds only. So if you're looking for exposure outside of what they offer (REITs, cryptocurrency, or commodities, which we cover in the next chapter), you may need to resort to doing that part yourself or hiring someone.

Most major brokerage firms have a robo-advisor option these days, and they offer retirement accounts like IRAs as well as regular taxable brokerage accounts.

The how-to of investment strategies

Now you know how important it is to invest and have this knowledge. You also know the three main ways to get invested (DIY, hire an advisor, or use a robo-advisor).

It's time to get into actual investment strategies in the next chapter and dive into how to use funds to construct a diversified portfolio easily.

Remember, your retirement plan is the blueprint, but investing represents the materials that actually build the retirement! This piece of the puzzle is essential to understand, even if it's just a base layer of knowledge.

Journal:

Circle which of the following statements best describes your investment attitude.

- I feel comfortable with stable investments.
- I am willing to withstand some fluctuations in my investment.
- I am seeking substantial investment returns.
- I am seeking potentially high investment returns.

What could prevent you from taking on more risk (e.g., having children/dependents, debt, health considerations)?

____

____

____

____

Do you want to be more of a hands-on investor, or a hands-off investor? What about a mix of both?

____

____

____

____

Chapter 8
Navigating Asset Classes and Investing Strategies

In the last chapter, we covered why you should have an investment strategy that fits your definition of financial freedom and your lifestyle.

Now we dive into the details a bit further in this chapter, to help you understand investing strategies on a deeper level. You may be able to go impress your family and friends with some of this information.

Keep in mind that the topic of investing runs wide and deep. I have hours upon hours of investing education content in my training course. For the scope of this book, I am not able to go into every detail, but this will give you a nice primer to start your journey.

The Top Asset Classes to Invest In

Before we get into investing strategies, let's take a look at the major asset classes that one can invest in and what they are.

1. Real Estate
2. Bonds
3. Equities
4. Commodities
5. Cryptocurrency

1. **Real Estate**

It's the most popular and well known asset class around. Many people in the United States actually hold the majority of their net worth in their home(s). Whether you have a personal residence or you're a real estate investor, your home can act as a store of value (one that helps beat inflation as asset prices rise) or an income stream if you decide to actively rent it out. I don't like to think of a primary home as an "investment" because of all of the costs associated with home ownership and occupation of it, but I do like to think of it as more of a "forced savings."

In retirement, you have hopefully paid your mortgage off after all those years, and as the housing prices increase, you may have a nice equity position in the home that helps bolster your net worth. Real estate investments are different; those are actively trying to earn you a positive return above your costs to hold the home.

If you're not into physical real estate, there is another way to get access by purchasing a financial security called a Real Estate Investment Trust (aka REIT). These are publicly traded companies that you can buy through any major brokerage. They invest in hard real estate across multiple industries on behalf of their investors (which would be you if you purchase shares of the REIT). They are legally obligated to pay out earnings, interest, and any capital gains they obtain from selling their properties, directly to their shareholders.

2. **Bonds**

You may remember your parents or grandparents buying you savings bonds as a gift when you were a kid. So, what actually is a bond? A bond is essentially you buying "debt" from another entity. Investors in bonds act like the "bank." In turn, the entity borrowing the money pays you interest and, eventually, you get your entire investment back (and you pocket the interest).

Think of a bond as you giving a loan to someone. Bonds are issued by corporations, federal governments, and municipalities (cities) for people like you and me (and institutions) to buy. They tend to be lower risk than stocks, but they definitely don't come without risk. The bond landscape is pretty wide and deep, but in a nutshell, entities are "graded" on how creditworthy they are to be getting "loans" from investors (think of it like a credit score). In other words, how likely are they to pay back the debt? Then, how likely they are to pay the debt will determine what kind of interest rate you may get as an investor.

Think about bonds in a similar way as getting a loan from the bank. The bank looks at our credit score and decides how worthy we are of their loan. With bonds, we investors are essentially the bank! Think of federal government (Treasury) bonds as the least risky. The idea behind this is that the government prints its own money and can never default on their debt.

Next up the line, think of municipalities (cities) as a bit more risky, but they do have the power to tax residents of their city to pay off debt on some types of bonds. But they can still see defaults, so many people look to higher quality cities that prove they can in fact pay their debts. Next, think of corporations. Corporations are split into investment grade (high credit quality with low chance of default) or junk bonds (lower credit quality companies with a higher chance of default, which will pay higher interest to you than investment grade bonds).

Every bond has a maturity date. The maturity date is when you will get your original investment back. Maturities can range from months (short-term) to many years (long-term).

3. **Equities (also known as stocks)**

Buying shares in a company is buying actual ownership in that company. You can own shares in publicly traded companies (think the public stock market), and you can even own shares in private companies (think investing in startups with venture capital or even your own company). Most people are investing in publicly traded companies that trade on well-known exchanges like the New York Stock Exchange or the NASDAQ exchange.

When a major corporation decides it wants to make its shares available to the public, it seeks an exchange to take its shares to the market for us to buy. This is an important concept to understand. The next major thing to know is what a stock index is, since many people are invested in funds (mutual funds or exchange traded funds) that actually track these indices!

The main stock indices are:

1. **The S&P 500 –** This tracks 500 of the largest U.S. companies by their size.
2. **The NASDAQ 100 –** This tracks 100 companies that trade on the NASDAQ exchange. They are technology-focused or growing revenues quickly.
3. **The Dow Jones Industrial Average –** This tracks 30 household names, and I personally tend to think it's not as useful as the S&P 500 due to the smaller number of companies it represents.

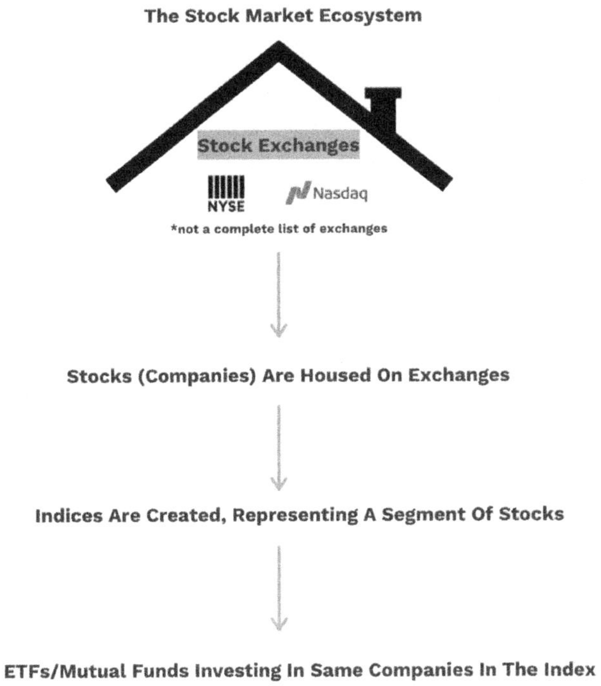

4. **Commodities**

These are materials that are used in everyday life or for manufacturing and agriculture, and you can invest in them. The most popular commodities to invest in are precious metals like gold, silver, and platinum. Then there is oil, which is an essential commodity in everyday life, as we use it to power our cities and our vehicles and manufacture everyday products.

There are also energy commodities like natural gas that are investable. Then you have other commodities like corn, lumber, and certain industrial metals like aluminum. Investments in this asset class tend to make up a smaller percentage of a portfolio because of the volatility that the prices can have, which increases overall risk. Commodities tend to be better investments during periods of high inflation.

5. **Cryptocurrency**

Cryptocurrency is a very new asset class, and it's debatable in the finance world if it's even an asset class at all or just one big speculative bubble. But let's set that aside for a moment. The most popular and largest cryptocurrency is Bitcoin. Bitcoin is essentially a decentralized (not controlled by any government or entity) digital currency that you can buy and sell goods and services with, but most people don't use it as a unit of exchange, and they hold it as an investment instead.

Taking into account the all-time-high of around $67,000 per coin, Bitcoin had a whopping over-100% annualized return PER YEAR since 2016. That means if you invested $1,000 dollars in 2016, it would, when averaged out over time, more than double every year if you held it. To put this into perspective, the S&P 500 (which tracks the top 500 companies in the U.S.)

has an average annual return of around 10%. So, however you lean here, the data has shown that popular cryptocurrencies seem to be sticking around and continuing to appreciate in value massively.

Of course, past performance doesn't predict future performance, and as (or if) it becomes more adopted in the future, professionals expect the returns and volatility to reduce and normalize.

Navigating the Different Ways to Invest in Asset Classes

So now you have an understanding of the main asset classes, but we have to take it a step further to figure out the landscape of "how" you can actually invest in these asset classes. This is where people tend to get confused, so don't feel bad if this section gets you asking questions (this is what my online training teaches in much more detail to help you understand it further since it's a topic with a lot of information surrounding it).

You can buy either of the following:

1. Individual assets
2. "Funds" that hold multiple individual assets

Individual assets include a physical house, individual stock in one specific company (shares of Apple or Google), an individual bond (issued by a government, municipality, or corporation), or an individual commodity like physical gold bars or oil futures (futures are outside the scope of this book, but if you're interested in investing in commodities, "futures contracts" are a good place to research next).

Funds are basically you buying one "fund" that holds multiple individual assets within it. Or a fund may even hold other funds in it (this is called a "fund of funds"). Think of funds as buying one box, but in that one box is a bunch of companies in the case of a stock fund. So, one purchase gets you everything you need, and it can get you instant diversification.

You can purchase individual stocks, bonds, or funds by opening a brokerage account. The brokerage account can be either taxable or a retirement account as we discussed in the prior chapters.

The most popular funds that people buy in their investing accounts (aka brokerage accounts) are mutual funds and exchange traded funds (ETFs). You may actually own funds without even knowing it. Most people who have a 401(k) at work, which, remember, is a type of retirement account held at a brokerage firm, own mutual funds or ETFs offered by their employer's plan. You just may not know because all of the investing happens automatically for you with employer-sponsored plans.

But I encourage you, if you do have a retirement plan at work or even an individual IRA, go check out what it is invested in. More importantly with individual retirement accounts (IRAs), you want to make sure the money you have contributed is actually invested in assets and is not just sitting in cash! With these accounts, it is our responsibility to invest the funds, unless you hire a money manager to do it for you, unlike employer-sponsored plans like 401(k)s.

Active vs. Passive Investing Methodology

So now that you understand your risk tolerance and capacity better from the prior chapter, it's time to take it a step further. There are a few ways you can invest. You can be a passive investor, an active investor, or a mix of both.

Passive investing is where you invest in funds like mutual funds or exchange traded funds (ETFs), which is like buying one box that is full of many different stocks, bonds, REITs, or a mix of other types of securities. The idea is to hold funds for a long period of time, let the interest or dividends reinvest, and grow your money in a very hands-off way.

Passive investing is wildly popular now, with brokers called robo-advisors now making it even easier. These robo-advisors will ask you some questions to get a feel for your risk tolerance and goals; then they'll automatically invest you in a diversified portfolio of ETFs.

Active investing is where you're actively researching and picking stocks. You're trying to manage your portfolio to deliver returns above and beyond what the stock indices like the S&P 500 or the NASDAQ 100 may do. In a nutshell, you're looking for the big bucks!

Active investing (aka "stock picking") has always been very appealing to people because, quite frankly, stock picking is fun, and many stocks have actually had insanely great returns (particularly technology stocks). However, it can be a losing game if you don't know what you're doing. Active investing requires you to understand how companies are valued and how to compare those values against those of other similar companies. As the famous investor Warren Buffett once said, "Price is what you pay. Value is what you get."

In other words, don't overpay!

Now, as far as active investing goes, there is plenty of data that shows most hedge fund managers who are picking stocks can't outperform the indices. However, I do think that stock picking done correctly, with the right strategy, can add value to a portfolio. This is where mixing both passive and active investing together comes into play. This is specifically what I do in my own portfolio.

I have the largest bulk of my portfolio passively invested in funds, and I actively invest a portion of it strategically. I do research, I compare valuations, and I invest in companies that I think have a long runway of growth ahead of them in interesting industries. Most people don't have the time or desire to do this research, and in that case, passive investing in funds does the job!

But if active investing interests you, a great way to use it, in my opinion, is to get more exposure to certain companies that only get a small allocation amount in your fund or companies that aren't represented in your fund at all.

Here is an example of that:

The following figure shows a popular core S&P 500 index fund, and you'll notice that the "% weight" column is different for many of the stocks descending from the highest allocation, which is Apple stock.

So, if you wanted a higher allocation than what is provided by the index for any of these companies, you could purchase some additional stock of the individual company you're interested in.

TICKER: IVV (iSHARES CORE S&P 500 ETF)

Ticker ▶	Name ▶	Sector ▶	Asset Class ▶	Market Value ▶	Weight (%) ▼
AAPL	APPLE INC	Information Technology	Equity	$16,463,568,311.64	5.79
MSFT	MICROSOFT CORP	Information Technology	Equity	$15,801,766,800.29	5.56
AMZN	AMAZON COM INC	Consumer Discretionary	Equity	$11,631,739,475.44	4.09
FB	FACEBOOK CLASS A INC	Communication	Equity	$6,468,899,416.14	2.27
GOOGL	ALPHABET INC CLASS A	Communication	Equity	$5,796,704,900.00	2.04
GOOG	ALPHABET INC CLASS C	Communication	Equity	$5,702,615,446.00	2.01
TSLA	TESLA INC	Consumer Discretionary	Equity	$4,121,658,243.94	1.45
BRKB	BERKSHIRE HATHAWAY INC CLASS B	Financials	Equity	$4,107,795,300.81	1.44
NVDA	NVIDIA CORP	Information Technology	Equity	$3,765,189,108.92	1.32
JPM	JPMORGAN CHASE & CO	Financials	Equity	$3,631,970,136.36	1.28

Source: iShares.com

COMPONENTS OF INVESTMENT STYLES AND FOCUS

It's time to dive into the heart of investing styles to help you construct a properly diversified portfolio.

Consider this: when you're going to the grocery store to buy some vegetables, it's not as simple as, "I'm going to buy vegetables." You have to drill it down to what KIND of vegetables you're going to buy. Will you buy root vegetables like potatoes, or are you wanting leafy green vegetables like lettuce or spinach? There are different "styles" of vegetables, and I want you to think of investing in assets to be the same idea.

Here are the main investing styles within asset classes that have more depth to them:

Real Estate

Residential - Think homes that families live in. This can be single family or multi-family homes like duplexes or apartments.

Commercial - This is property used by businesses. From stand-alone property to strip malls and larger buildings.

Land - Many people invest in land in areas that they think will grow in the future. (Fun fact: You can't depreciate land like you can the property on it!)

Equity (stocks/businesses)

Value - Value stocks are considered to be trading at lower valuations than what they're actually worth. The idea with value stocks is that the market is "missing something," and there is an opportunity for the stock price to appreciate to what it's worth.

Growth - Growth stocks tend to be more expensive than value stocks. You are essentially paying a "premium" for a company that is growing revenues at higher rates than a value company might be doing. Growth stocks are usually newer companies in innovating industries and tend to be higher risk than value stocks. Many growth stocks over the past decade have been in the technology sector.

Domestic - Domestic stocks are getting you shares of companies that are in the United States.

International - International stocks are getting you shares of companies that are outside of the United States (this can be any country).

Emerging - Emerging markets are in up-and-coming countries that haven't quite developed from an economical and technological perspective as much as first world countries have. China is a great example of what has been and can still be considered an emerging market. There are many emerging countries that you can invest in. You'd be investing in the businesses associated with those countries. Emerging markets tend to have geopolitical and currency risks to keep in mind, but there is usually an opportunity for growth that exists in their economies and in their middle class (bringing people out of poverty). Some countries that emerging market funds tend to invest in are Brazil, Mexico, Indonesia, Thailand, and others.

Developed - Developed markets are the opposite of emerging markets. These are countries that are considered "first world" countries like the United States, Canada, Germany, Australia, the United Kingdom, and others. There is less risk in investing in developed countries versus emerging ones.

Thematic - Thematic investing is buying stock in companies or funds that fit a certain theme. This could be investing in a fund that invests in only gaming stocks, or renewable energy stocks, or financial technology stocks, for example. I would consider thematic investing to be a smaller part of a portfolio versus your entire portfolio being invested in one or two themes.

The idea is to have diversification across multiple styles of investing (and potentially multiple geographical regions) that suits your risk tolerance.

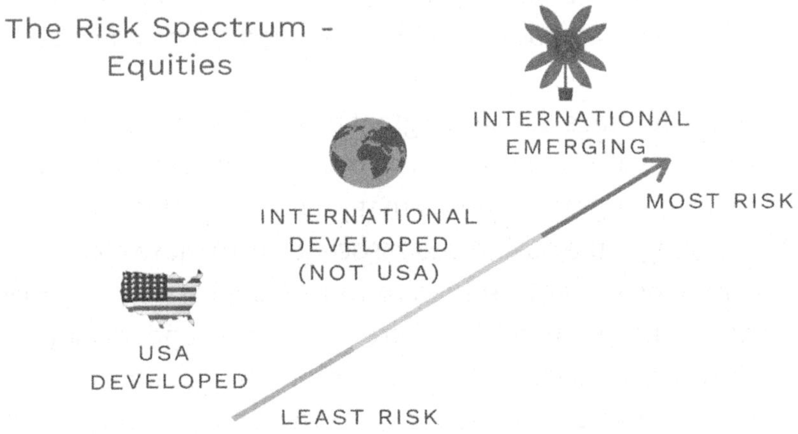

Source: She Talks Finance Training Program

Putting it all together as shown above: you can have a value stock that represents shares of a company that is international (outside the U.S.) and in an emerging market (like India or Brazil).

Bonds (debt)

Investment Grade Corporate Bonds – Just like we get a credit score to be able to take out a loan from the bank, corporations also get graded on how creditworthy they are. Investment grade bonds are you investing in the debt of some of the best companies who are more likely to pay back their debts to you as an investor. These bonds usually pay lower interest rates to investors (similarly to how you pay a lower interest rate on a mortgage if you have good credit).

High-Yield Corporate Bonds (aka Junk Bonds) – Beware of junk bonds, because although they pay higher interest rates than investment grade bonds, these are companies with lower credit quality. So they're more likely to default on their debt. This doesn't mean they will, of course, and investors with a higher risk tolerance typically don't mind taking on the risk to get paid a higher interest rate.

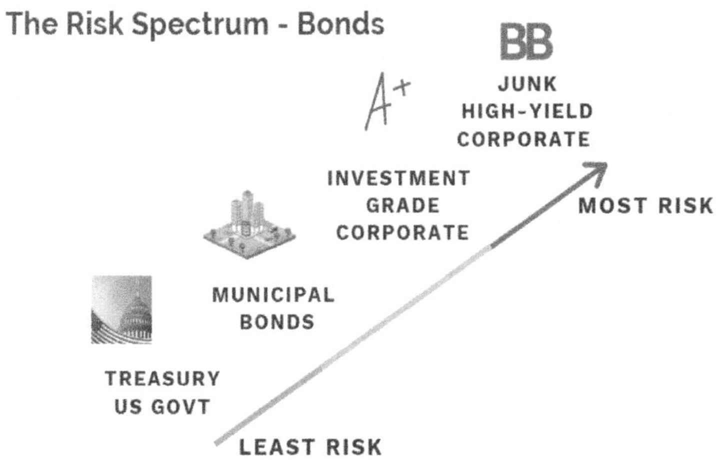

Source: She Talks Finance Training Program

Investment Allocations Make the Portfolio

Putting together a portfolio can sound like a daunting task, but it's actually more simple than you think with the availability of funds that we have these days!

The big idea with portfolio allocation is balancing taking on the right amount of risk for the right amount of return to reach your goals. Keep in mind, markets go up and down, and downturns will very likely happen while you're invested. (However, I actually see these downturns in the market as opportunities to go "shopping" and buy more stocks!)

Remember, the idea is to allocate a portfolio in a way that keeps you in the game long-term!

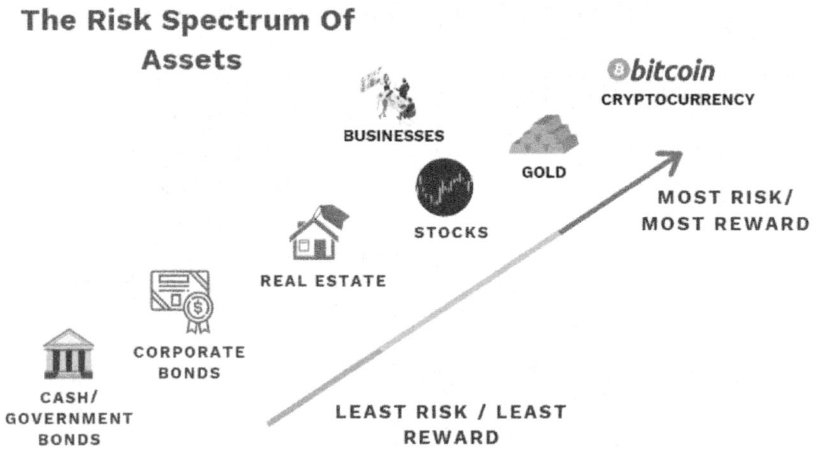

Source: She Talks Finance Training Program

Think of the amount you're looking to invest as a pie ... and you're going to be filling up that pie with different percentages of different types of assets.

The main idea is someone who is very risk averse and hates losing money should not have a portfolio allocation of mostly cryptocurrency and commodities (like gold). As you can see on the risk spectrum above, those are the highest risk assets (risk = how much an asset can go down in price compared to others)!

Here are some example portfolio allocations based on different types of risk.

In this case, I'll use all of the broad asset classes; however, there are some things to keep in mind when looking at these example allocations:

- These are just examples for educational purposes and should not be relied upon as the right allocations for YOU.
- You absolutely do not have to invest in all of the asset classes. Feel free to leave any asset class out that you're uncomfortable being invested in.
- I will list broad asset classes, but keep in mind that within that allocation, you can break it up between different styles of investing (growth/value/large-cap/mid-cap/small-cap/thematic), geographical regions (domestic versus international), and developed versus emerging markets.
- Anywhere you see "other" as an allocation is typically where you can put in smaller allocations of things like municipal bonds, real estate, commodities, or crypto-currencies. These types of assets do not typically make up large allocations in a portfolio.

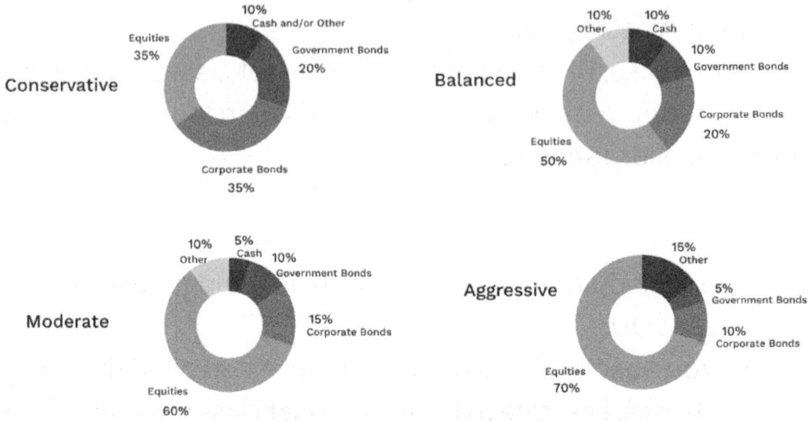

Source: She Talks Finance

Now something important to keep in mind is that your allocations can and should change as you age. When you're young, you're in the accumulation stage of wealth, so you may have a more aggressive allocation. However, as you get older, you move into the preservation stage of wealth, and you need to move into a more conservative allocation to keep the wealth you've built safer for use in retirement!

Investing in Funds: The Essential Details

Here are some of the main takeaways around funds and different asset classes that may help you learn how to better construct a portfolio when it's time.

Real estate

There are funds that invest in individual companies that are in the real estate business (think homebuilders or online marketplaces like Zillow). There are also funds that invest in a group of Real Estate Investment Trusts (REITs). There are REITs that own real estate and operate across multiple industries, and you can find funds specifically for a certain industry like retirement communities, apartment complexes, or retail, for example.

Bonds

Bonds can get very complex, so the nitty-gritty details are beyond the scope of this book. But I'll certainly give you some good takeaways here to consider.

There are a variety of bond funds that invest in treasury bonds, muni bonds (municipality-issued bonds), or corporate bonds. There are also funds that invest in a mix of all of these to some degree (for broad, diversified exposure).

The most important things to consider with bonds are:

- **What is the average maturity of the bond fund?** Maturity is the date you're expected to get paid back your original investment. By the time maturity comes, you would have gotten paid all of your interest along the way. But keep in mind that the price of a bond security can change in between when it's issued and when its maturity comes. So, if a fund sells a bond earlier than its maturity date, there is a possibility of loss on that bond. The shorter average maturity of a bond fund usually means it's less volatile, and the interest rate tends to be lower because you're taking on less risk (your money is not "locked up" long). The longer the average maturity of a bond fund, the more volatile it can be, and the higher the interest rate usually is (you're typically "rewarded" with a higher rate for locking up your money long-term). However, this dynamic can change!

- **What is the interest rate your bond is currently paying?** The interest rate will change as the price of the bond changes. There is something called the 30-Day SEC Yield that you'll find when researching bond funds. This is telling you how much you can expect to earn on the bond fund, taking into account expenses, assuming nothing changes.

Equities (stocks)

The main idea with equity funds is to know what mix of the following exists in the fund:

1. Large capitalization stocks
2. Mid capitalization stocks
3. Small capitalization stocks
4. Developed versus Emerging markets
5. Domestic versus International companies
6. Growth versus Value stocks

Some funds are just core index funds tracking only the large capitalization stocks in the S&P 500 or NASDAQ, and others have a mix of literally everything I just mentioned above! So not all equity funds are equal.

To help you make sense of this, here is an ETF from Vanguard that represents how a fund can have all of the above in it.

This is the Vanguard Total World Stock Market ETF (Ticker: VT)

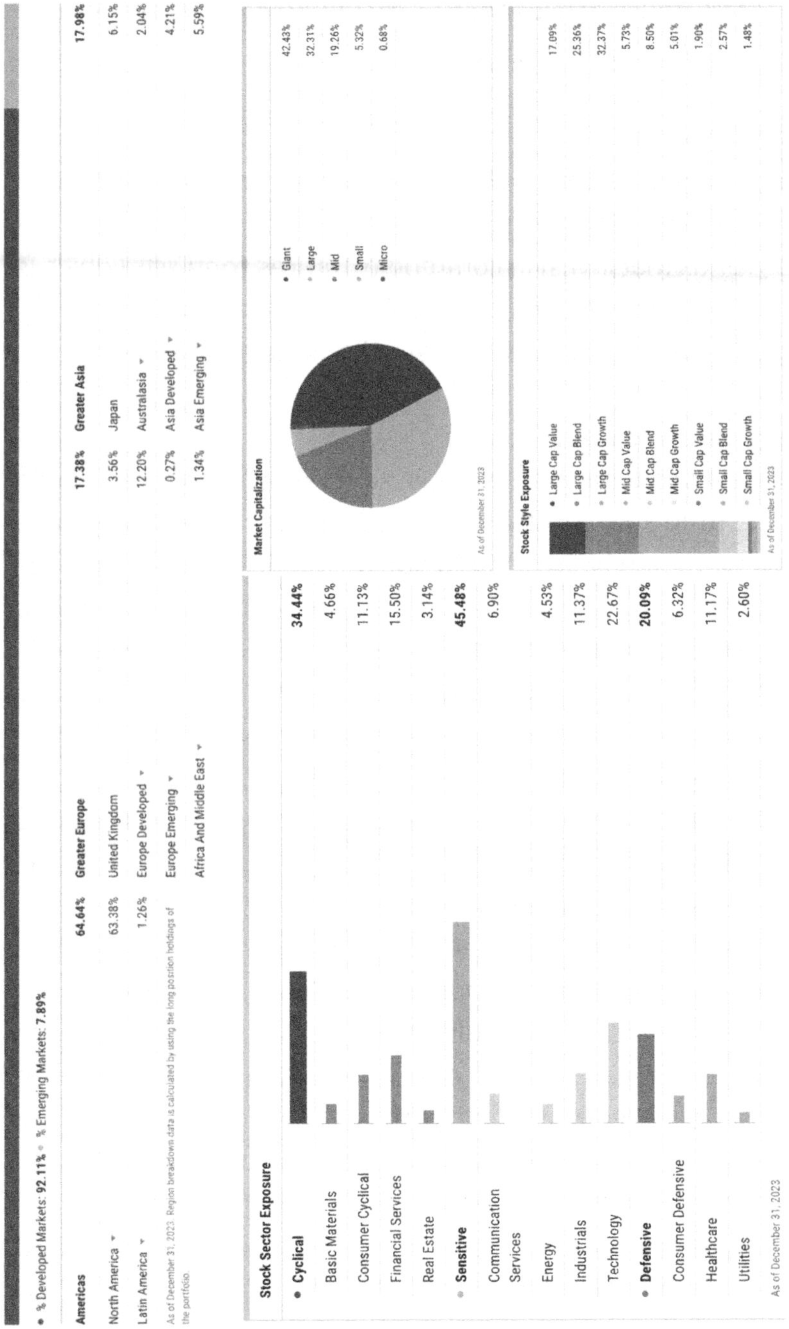

Source: Ycharts.com (Image turned sideways for better visibility)

You'll notice that it's got a bit of everything across geographical regions, styles, and sectors.

Commodities

There are funds that invest in companies that are involved in the discovery and production of commodities, and there are also funds that invest in commodity futures contracts (which is beyond the scope of this book). The most popular commodity funds have been ETFs that track the price of gold or oil.

Cryptocurrencies

This is a pretty new asset class, so there isn't much available in the fund space outside of one company called Grayscale. However, we have seen ETFs pop up that invest in companies involved in blockchain technology. We've also seen multiple investment firms submit for a Bitcoin ETF to be approved, but, so far, we haven't seen one in the United States. Many financial professionals are expecting it to eventually happen. There's a fund for this, and this ... and that.

If you can think of some way you want to invest, the odds are, there is a fund out there (mutual fund or ETF) that will offer you what you're looking for.

Want to invest in just the S&P 500 index, which represents the largest 500 U.S. companies? There is a fund for that. Want to invest in a fund that holds both stocks and bonds? There is a fund for that. You can even invest via a fund in a specific industry like retail, gaming, or software. Or say you want to get exposure to companies in a certain country, like India? Yep, you guessed it, there is a fund for that too.

So, as you can imagine, this topic can get really wide and deep, but don't let that overwhelm you. In the next chapter, we're going to dive deeper into investing strategies via funds.

If you're interested in poking around at different fund types just to get a grasp on some of the topics I have written about, here are a few websites from the top fund providers to look at. Again, keep in mind that the next chapter will help a lot of this come together.

You can search through the fund provider's offerings and filter by what you're looking to invest in. In fact, I think poking around at the fund offerings BEFORE you dive into the next chapter might be helpful to get some of the terms in your consciousness.

Mutual funds & ETFs

BlackRock: https://www.ishares.com/us
Vanguard: https://investor.vanguard.com/home
Fidelity: https://www.fidelity.com
Charles Schwab: https://www.schwab.com

Mutual fund focused

American Funds: https://americanfundsretirement.retire.americanfunds.com
Dimensional Funds: https://us.dimensional.com/funds

Keep in mind that there are many different fund providers, and if you're in a retirement plan at work, you'll be likely subject to whatever provider they give you access to (and different funds versus if you were investing on your own in your IRA). When investing in your own account, you have a lot of flexibility about which fund providers you can invest with.

If You're Still Overwhelmed ... Do This, and Then Re-read These Chapters

Investing is a deep subject that can be very nuanced if you go far enough into it. Even after a class, I hear from people who say that their eyes are opened, but they're still feeling a little overwhelmed with it all.

I encourage people to take investing one subject matter at a time. Master what a brokerage account is, then move on to understanding stock indices like the S&P 500 and the NASDAQ.

Once you have that down, then move into poking around the different fund sites I provided in the last section. Take a look at the holdings in the funds and the cost of the fund (aka the expense ratio) and compare it to others. Go peek at your retirement plan at work to find out what it is invested in (then, look up that fund!).

The more you poke around here, the more it will make sense. This is the best way to learn about investing.

Once you've mastered funds, then you can move into more advanced topics like individual stock picking and more.

Now, we move on from investing to a topic everyone loves to hate: taxes! Don't skip it, though, considering taxes are one of our largest expenses in our lives.

JOURNAL:

What asset classes are you most interested in investing in, and why?

Part V

Keeping More Of Your Money ... Legally

Chapter 9
Taxes: Your Biggest Life Expense

Disclaimer: Tax laws are always changing. Be sure to check IRS.gov for the most up to date tax information.

TAXES

The word alone sends many people running the other way toward a bottle of wine. Others may not be too bothered by paying taxes.

Taxes creep up in many ways in our lives though. Social Security, Medicare, state, local, sales, and federal taxes are the most common ones paid.

Surprisingly, taxes end up being many people's largest expense paid over their lifetime, and yet I find it is one of the least understood topics broadly. My tax content is my most under-liked content on social media. I get it, though; taxes seem impossible to understand. And boring.

You may be thinking that you don't need to really understand taxes. Maybe you have an accountant, or maybe you just do your taxes online, and the simplicity doesn't trigger you to research taxes deeper. But in the next few chapters, you're going to learn why it can be essential to understand your taxes.

Before I lose you, being aware of your tax situation and strategizing doesn't require you to be an accountant ... so, I hope you stick through these next few chapters, because they could save you thousands of dollars over your lifetime.

I have found that no matter your tax situation, there is almost always room for strategizing here to reach your definition of financial freedom.

You work hard to earn your money, so you have the right to understand how one of the largest expenses in your life works! Right?!

How I Went from Knowing Nothing About Tax ... to Loving Tax

I have to admit that I am a nerd for tax planning. There is nothing more satisfying than realizing you can save thousands of dollars on your tax bill or knowing the rules that help you avoid taxation altogether in some scenarios.

It wasn't always like this for me, though. I started running a small business with my husband after I quit corporate America, and I didn't know much at all about taxes. I had been employed, and they took out taxes from my paycheck, and I would get a refund at the end of the year (but I didn't quite understand why). That was about the extent of my tax knowledge.

I feel that most people are in this scenario. (I later found out that a tax refund isn't actually a good thing. You're just giving the government an interest-free loan. More on this later.)

It wasn't until I started working with an accountant for our business that I was running that I realized I had a lot to learn.

When our business showed a profit, the tax bills were a shock to me. "I have to cut a check for how much?" I'd say. Not a bad problem to have, but it really threw me into the world of tax strategy.

I would ask questions on how to reduce my tax bill, but accountant explanations would go in one ear and out the other. I'd do whatever they told me to do, like deposit money into an IRA to get a tax deduction, but I had no idea what I was actually doing with my money or truly why.

As it turns out, I was putting money into retirement accounts like they told me to do to save money on taxes, but I didn't know that it would stay uninvested unless I had someone manage my money for me or invested it myself! Otherwise, it was just sitting in cash in my account not participating in the benefits of investing at all! This is a common story for many people, I have learned!

Accountants can tell you ways to reduce your tax bill, and that may be contributing to a retirement account, but they cannot advise you on *how* to invest the money unless they are a registered investment advisor. So, you may follow their advice, but there may be more steps you need to take.

This is the problem with being told what to do without *actually* understanding what you're doing. At least it was a problem for me.

Of course, I didn't want to ask too many more questions at first because I didn't want to sound stupid ... but then, as things went on, I got tired of not truly understanding my tax situation or, quite frankly, anything they would tell me to do.

After a few CPAs, I finally found one who would break down taxes for me in a much clearer way. He became more of a mentor, and this is actually why I decided to get my CERTIFIED FINANCIAL PLANNER™ designation. He was a *tax strategist*. He sat down with me whenever I needed and thoroughly explained why we were doing the strategies we were doing.

The more I learned, the more I loved the "art" of tax strategy. Even more, I realized that yes, our tax code in the United States is incredibly complicated. However, it's possible, with a solid overview, to understand how to do better planning for yourself.

Why Understanding Your Tax Situation Is So Important

You may be thinking to yourself, *Nikki, I have an accountant who does all of this for me; I don't need to know what's happening.*

Well, you may be right, you may have a wonderful accountant, but I have a story or two for you.

What I have learned during my years in finance is that not all accountants are created equal. There are many very talented tax professionals providing great service. However, there are others who may only have one way of approaching it: take your tax documents, plug in the numbers, and spit out what you owe or what your tax refund is. They offer no tips for reducing your tax bill, no matter how simple or obvious that tip may be.

Ideally, you want your tax professional or financial planner to be asking you the right questions that lead them to the right tax-saving strategies.

If you're not working with a tax professional, you're likely doing your taxes on your own via a website like TurboTax or H&R Block. You get your tax documents and plug the numbers in accordingly in the software. This is totally fine!

However, that's even more reason for you to read through these chapters and get a better grasp on taxation so that you don't make any major mistakes. You don't know what you don't know about tax. For the do-it-yourself tax preparer, these chapters are imperative.

As far as tax horror stories go, I've talked about Roth IRAs in prior chapters. The Roth IRA is a specific type of account where you can't contribute to it if you have too much income. If you do, you will owe a 6% penalty every year that the ineligible contributions are left in the IRA. I know of multiple people who made too much money, didn't know the rules, and made ineligible Roth IRA contributions. Their accountants never mentioned it to them, so they didn't know any better until they found out they owed thousands of dollars in penalties. It's not a fun process to undo the mistake of ineligible Roth contributions over many years.

I've also heard stories of accountants not taking into account certain deductions that the individual was entitled to. Or not asking qualifying questions that would help a client avoid a tax bill altogether on sales of certain assets like homes or small business stock (more on this later).

Here's another story about a good friend and his spouse, who are self-employed. He was talking to me about his tax bill and asking me why it was so high and what he could do to lower it (keep in mind, self-employed individuals don't have someone taking taxes out of their paycheck automatically like you do at a job where you get a W-2). I asked him a few questions about his and his spouse's business, and a few other questions. I took a peek at the tax return and was horrified at what I saw.

The accountant had been reporting their income incorrectly for their business structure, and he did not recommend the right type of retirement account for them to save more money on their tax bill. They wanted to completely max out retirement contributions beyond what their current account allowed. My friend had overpaid thousands of dollars on taxes due to this oversight on the accountant's part. I immediately told him how he should be structuring how he is paid from his business, and the right type of retirement account to use, and I suggested he find another tax professional.

My friend later told me that he ended up hiring a new one, and he told him to do exactly what I had told him, which made him feel comfortable. His old accountant had been filing his taxes completely inefficiently (and he was a Certified Public Accountant).

The point is not for you to be a whiz and know everything about tax. That's impossible and not even accountants know everything about tax (but they know how to find things out).

It's simply being aware of some of the big ideas so that you can have a productive conversation with your tax professional and even do planning for yourself before you talk to your tax professional.

This is a very big recurring theme you may see in my content. I believe that knowledge is power and can help you be sure nothing goes unnoticed.

What Is a Tax Refund, Anyway?

If you're like most people who work for an employer, you fill out a W-4 form that your employer gives you to determine how much tax they should withhold from your paycheck. You then receive a W-2 at the end of the year showing how much you've made and how much tax was withheld.

Your employer is withholding taxes from every paycheck and actually sending that money to the IRS on your behalf. Side note: Those who are self-employed (this includes you if you're a 1099 contractor) are responsible for sending in estimated tax payments quarterly, as there is no employer withholding taxes for you!

An employee who is single with no kids may request, via their W-4 form, to have their employer withhold more taxes from their paycheck than someone who has a lot of dependents. This is because many people with dependents get tax credits to help lower their tax liability. The W-4 form is where this information is relayed to the employer so that they know how much to take out.

You may do your taxes the next year and happily get a tax refund check from the IRS.

This is usually an exciting time for people, and tax-refund time is practically celebrated in the United States.

Tax refunds are not "extra money" ... getting one means you overpaid the IRS after all of your deductions and credits were accounted for on your final tax return. It's your money originally, from your paycheck, which you essentially lent to the IRS interest-free.

I will follow that statement up with this ... tax refunds can be seen as "forced savings." If saving money isn't your strong suit, then your employer withholding more taxes from your paycheck may not be the worst thing for you. You get it back eventually, and it's almost like the IRS is your savings account.

But here's the flip side of that coin ... think about what you could have done with that tax refund money throughout the year instead of the IRS holding onto it. You could have maybe paid down some higher interest debt (and saved money on interest). You could have bolstered your savings (that is actually earning some interest in a high-yield savings account). You could have even gotten that money invested! Remember, the sooner money gets into the stock market, the better over time.

Time can be of the essence, and the money may have been better in your hands throughout the year rather than in the IRS's hands.

Legally Manipulating Your Tax Refund or Bill

So what are you supposed to actually do here about a tax refund? Maybe you want to increase your refund one year, or perhaps you don't want a huge refund and you'd like more of your money in your pocket today instead of the IRS "holding onto it."

Well, keep in mind that your tax refund or how much you owe can be changed depending on a number of things: how you contribute to retirement, if in a given year you have kids, start a business, or sell a business or an asset, to name a few things.

If You're Employed, Update Your W-4

My first suggestion if you're employed is to check your W-4 (especially if you have added a dependent since you filled it out), and maybe ask your employer if you can fill out a new one.

There is a special tool on the IRS website that I highly suggest you go through to make sure you're having the right amount of money withheld, but not TOO much to the point you're giving the IRS that tax-free loan all year.

This tool is called the Tax Withholding Estimator, and you can find it on IRS.gov. It takes into account your specific situation and can help give you an idea of how much your employer should be withholding. You can then make adjustments from there if you need to through your employer.

Now, what about "legally manipulating" your tax refund or bill?

Retirement Accounts for Legal Tax Savings

The most common way to "legally manipulate" your tax refund is to increase contributions to your "traditional" retirement accounts. This could be a Traditional IRA, Traditional 401(k), 403(b), or eligible 457(b). If you're self-employed, traditional accounts would be a SEP-IRA or a Solo-401(k).

Notice I didn't say Roth IRA or Roth 401(k)? I said "traditional." This is a key distinction.

If you recall, traditional accounts give you a federal tax deduction NOW, and you pay taxes in retirement when you pull the money out. Roth account contributions do not give you a tax deduction today, so taxes can't be reduced today by contributing to a Roth.

So, if you contribute to any of these traditional (non-Roth) accounts, you end up reducing your taxable income, and in turn, increasing a tax refund or reducing a tax bill if you're self-employed.

I'll cover shortly how to make the decision between contributing to a traditional retirement account versus a Roth account. It's not always the wisest decision to take the traditional route, depending on a few factors.

Also keep in mind that there are income limitations to deducting specifically to a Traditional IRA if you or your spouse has access to a retirement plan at work.

Getting the Basics of Taxes Down

I will dive into how taxes are actually calculated in the next chapter. This knowledge comes in handy when you're trying to decide how much you should or shouldn't contribute to retirement and if you're trying to qualify for certain tax deductions.

But, in this section, I want to cover the big ideas that you need to know when it comes to tax strategy.

This will help you when it comes time to read the tax calculation section (don't be afraid, it's simpler than you think with the way I break it down!).

We've covered the biggest idea over a few chapters about "traditional" versus "Roth" accounts, and we will talk in the next section about how to make the choice between the two.

As for some other big ideas in the tax world, here is a short list:

1. **Itemized versus standard deduction:** A deduction is an amount that helps lower your overall tax liability. If you own a business, you can deduct business expenses from your income (in addition to other deductions on your personal return, like a standard deduction). Everyone who files taxes gets to choose between taking a standard deduction amount that the government sets for us (a "discount" on our taxes, if you will), or you itemizing your deductions like mortgage interest, property taxes, charitable deductions, and more. You can't do both. You want to figure out which dollar amount

allows you a larger tax deduction: the standard deduction or itemizing deductions (like your property taxes and mortgage interest, for example). I'll touch on this more in the next chapter.

2. **Effective versus marginal tax rates:** If one year you get a smaller tax refund or owe more taxes than normal, before you get upset, find out what the effective tax rate was that you actually paid and compare it. An effective rate is your average tax rate paid. This rate is found by dividing your taxes paid by your taxable income. On the other hand, there is your marginal tax rate. This is simply the highest tax rate you pay on the last dollar of your income (we have a progressive tax system where your income moves through multiple "brackets.") You'll learn about this more in the next chapter.
3. **Tax deductions:** Deductions are used to reduce your taxable income; therefore they reduce your tax liability. Business owners typically utilize deductions the most when coming up with their net income to start their tax calculation, but there are deductions that could apply to anyone. Some of the most popular deductions that people itemize on their taxes are property taxes and mortgage interest paid for their homes, charitable contributions, and healthcare expenses above a certain percentage of your income (rules apply). Note that if your itemized deductions aren't more than the standard deduction, then you may be doing yourself a disservice by not choosing the standard deduction! Tax software is pretty good at snuffing this out for you.
4. **Tax credits:** There are many tax credits offered by the government. There are credits for taking care of

dependents, having children, making a lower income, paying for college, healthcare credits, and more. Credits reduce your tax bill dollar for dollar and are applied once your tax due is calculated. Some tax credits are "fully refundable," and even after your tax bill is reduced to zero, you can get additional money back.

The Traditional versus Roth Conundrum

Now back to retirement accounts. Choosing between traditional and Roth retirement contributions can be confusing for some people, but I hope to simplify this for you a bit.

Which account you should choose depends on a few things:

1. **What your effective tax rate is today:** Find out what your tax rate paid is first so that you can make an informed decision. The typical rule of thumb is the lower your tax rate, the more you should lean toward a Roth account. You're locking in a low tax rate today to get tax-free growth later in a Roth. On the flip side, the higher your tax rate is, especially anything in the top two tax brackets, the more you may want to lean toward a traditional account to get the tax deduction today (and some relief from those top tax rates).
2. **What you believe tax rates will look like in the future:** There are a lot of unknowns in tax-land today and in the future. Congress can change rules as the years go, and depending on central bank monetary and governmental fiscal policies, that could mean similar or more taxation for our future selves. So a lot of the choice between traditional or Roth relies

upon your own beliefs about what taxes may look like in the future. If you're convinced that we'll be staring higher tax rates down in the future, you may be more inclined to use a Roth account. (Fun fact: Roth IRAs have income limits that may make you ineligible, but Roth 401(k) accounts do not.)

3. **If you need a lower tax bill:** Maybe you actually need to keep more money in a given year for a specific reason. If so, maybe you simply need as many deductions as you can get. In that case, you may want to consider a traditional account.

Tax Timing Is Queen

As I mentioned, we have a lot of unknowns ahead of us, so no one can strategize taxes perfectly. This is why I really love tax timing.

This is simply using both traditional and Roth accounts, on and off, depending on your income every year (aka tax timing).

Maybe one year, you have lower income, and you're going to pay a lower tax rate. Why not take advantage of Roth in that year and lock in a nice low tax rate? The money you invest in here will grow tax-free for you later.

Or maybe you have a big year in your business or get a huge bonus at work. Maybe this would be a good year to take advantage of a traditional account and reduce the tax hit a little bit.

In the end, you end up with a nice mix of both types of accounts, which can come in handy in retirement for controlling your income (you can pull from Roth in retirement when you need to keep income low since qualified distributions [aka withdrawals] are not considered income for tax purposes like a Traditional IRA).

There is also the great benefit in a Roth account of not being required to take distributions from it at a certain age (the government wants their tax money, so they force distributions from traditional accounts by 73 years old as of this writing—it's called a "required minimum distribution").

So don't think of the decision as having to be one or the other forever! You can even contribute to both in the same year up to certain total limits.

So tax diversifying (aka tax timing) helps take the stress out of having to predict what taxes will look like in the future, while giving you flexibility later in retirement!

Diving into the Details

In the next chapter, we're going to dive into the details behind how taxes are actually calculated (the flow of taxation), which will help you learn how to properly strategize going forward.

We will cover some of the top tax strategies that most people can actually take advantage of.

Journal:

Go find your latest tax return. Let's calculate your effective (average) tax rate. All good tax planning starts here!

Step 1: Find your 1040 form. This is the main form for your tax return.

Step 2: Find the line that says "**Taxable Income**."

Step 3: Find the line that says "**Total Tax**."

Step 4: Divide the "**Total Tax**" line by the "**Taxable Income**" line. This gives you your average tax rate (aka effective rate).

Write your effective tax rate here:

Chapter 10
Tax Strategies for More Wealth

Disclaimer: Tax laws are always changing. Be sure to check on IRS.gov for the most up to date tax information.

In the last chapter I explained why understanding your tax situation is so important.

I also briefly covered how you can easily manipulate your tax bill by contributing to traditional retirement accounts and why that may not be the best choice depending on your effective tax rate (average rate).

Now, we get into what they should have taught us all in school: how taxes are calculated.

Don't Be Afraid ... I'm About to Walk You Through Taxation

It is now time for you to learn how taxation works before we get into tax strategies.

This is going to be a general overview to keep things simple! So, just know that there may be intricacies not mentioned, but this is a great overall picture of taxation. Here is the image that will be followed by descriptions of each step.

I suggest viewing the image now, again as I walk through each line, and then again at the end of this section. (Repetition is key with this stuff!)

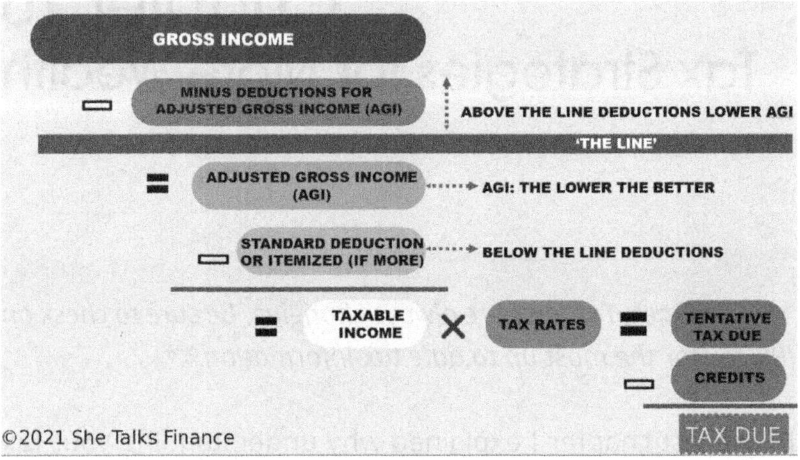

Taxation starts with **gross income**. This is what you make before any taxes and before deductions for retirement plans or health insurance come from your paycheck.

From there, it's time to start subtracting what we call **"above the line deductions."** These are the best kind of deductions because they really help get our **adjusted gross income (AGI)** down. You want your AGI low because much tax credit eligibility is based on a version of your AGI.

*Here are the **main** types of **"above the line" deductions** that lead us eventually to a lower AGI:*

1. Self-employed health insurance
2. Half of your self-employed taxes paid as a deduction (since when you're self-employed, you pay both the employee and employer halves of Social Security and

Medicare tax, this is supposed to help level the playing field)
3. Business expenses if you're self-employed
4. Retirement plan contributions (traditional only, no deduction for Roth contributions)
5. Capital losses on investments up to a limit
6. Student loan interest up to a limit
7. Health Savings Account contributions

So, now, your **above the line deductions** are subtracted from your **gross income** which leads you to your official **adjusted gross income (AGI).**

The next step is more deductions, but this time, these are **"below the line deductions"** that happen after your AGI is calculated.

You get the choice of either a **standard deduction** that the government allows anyone to take ($14,600 for single or $29,200 for married as of this writing) OR **itemized deductions**.

Whichever amount is higher is the one you want to take!

So itemized deductions are the **"below the line deductions"** that I am talking about. These might consist of:

1. Charitable contributions (to qualified 501(c) charities)
2. Property, state, or local taxes paid (rules apply)
3. Mortgage interest (rules apply)
4. Medical expenses that are over a certain percentage of your AGI (another reason to have lower AGI!)

So, for example, if you're single, and you end up having property taxes, charitable contributions, and mortgage interest deductions, but their total amount is not higher than the

$14,600 standard deduction, you're better off just taking the standard deduction. (See the IRS.gov website for the most updated standard deduction number.)

Now, after subtracting your **below the line deduction** (either the standard or itemized deduction), you're left with your actual **taxable income**.

The next step is that your taxable income is multiplied by the tax rates. Notice I said rates, plural. Keep in mind that our tax system is progressive, so our taxable income moves through multiple tax brackets unless you make very low income. The more income you make, the more tax brackets your income moves through.

This is why we care more about an EFFECTIVE (average) tax rate! Because some of our income is taxed at lower rates and some at higher rates. It's not all or nothing here.

Understanding Tax Brackets

A huge misconception is that making more money will "bump you into a higher tax bracket." The truth is, only SOME of your money will be bumped into a higher bracket, not all of it!

Here is what our tax brackets look like as of this writing for single and married individuals:

Tax Rate	Taxable income bracket
10%	$0 to $11,600.
12%	$11,601 to $47,150.
22%	$47,151 to $100,525.
24%	$100,526 to $191,950.
32%	$191,951 to $243,725.
35%	$243,726 to $609,350.
37%	$609,351 or more.

Source: Single Filer Tax Brackets NerdWallet.com

Note: These rates and figures are as of 2024 and may change.

Tax rate	Taxable income bracket
10%	$0 to $23,200.
12%	$23,201 to $94,300.
22%	$94,301 to $201,050.
24%	$201,051 to $383,900.
32%	$383,901 to $487,450.
35%	$487,451 to $731,200.
37%	$731,201 or more.

Source: Married Filing Jointly Tax Brackets NerdWallet.com

Note: These rates and figures are as of 2024 and may change.

So, by looking at these tax tables, I hope you can see that not all of your income is taxed at the same rate!

A good example of how our progressive tax system works is looking at a single person making $60,000 in taxable income (not AGI, but actually taxable income).

If you look at the tax table above for a single filer, you'll see that $60,000 of taxable income puts them in the 22% tax bracket.

But only $12,850 of that $60,000 income would actually be taxed at 22%. The previous amount moved through the 10% and 12% brackets and was taxed accordingly. $11,600 of the $60,000 was taxed at 10% and then $35,550 of the $60,000 was taxed at 12%. This left the rest of the $12,850 of income to be taxed at that 22% rate.

Now, what if she could have avoided bumping into that 22% rate by contributing that $12,850 amount to her Traditional 401(k) at work instead (assuming she's within the annual 401(k) contribution limit)?

She would have had an above the line deduction that helped lower her tax liability and keep the last of her income in that 12% bracket. Her taxable income would have been $12,850 less. Going from 12% to 22% is quite a jump, so tax savings here could have been over $2,827 ($12,850 multiplied by that 22% tax rate)

Granted, this is just an example, and a 22% tax rate isn't all that bad actually if you believe taxes will be much higher in the future. This could warrant a Roth contribution instead ... but I hope you get the point here!

And this, my friend, is why it's important to understand how taxes are calculated and your tax situation!

If you're looking like a deer in headlights right now, feeling confused, don't worry. That's normal. I go into these details in video format in my training program, and it really helps to hear me walk through it. But this at least gives you a primer on the terms and flow of taxation (and the idea of lowering your tax liability by pulling levers like retirement contributions).

Tax Strategies

Some of the top strategies used by financial professionals include Roth conversions, proper asset location, and controlling income to avoid taxation.

I'm going to touch on these in more detail in this section.

Roth conversions

Roth conversion is one of the most used strategies to reduce taxation over your lifetime. This isn't about instant gratification today. This is about strategy over the long haul. A Roth conversion is where you take money in a traditional retirement account, and you convert it into a Roth account. Money that is converted is added to your tax return as income, and you pay taxes on it. You may be thinking, *Why would I do that and increase my income?*

You'd do this if you will be in a lower, more attractive tax bracket that you'd like to lock in today (you pay tax now, to avoid higher taxes later). If you have a year with less income, or even no income, it can make sense to do a conversion in that year since you're likely to have a very low effective (average) tax rate.

There is a rule called the pro-rata rule to watch out for when doing conversions if you have a Traditional IRA that has **both** pre- and post-tax money in it, and you don't plan to convert the entire IRA. I suggest using the help of a Certified Public Accountant (CPA) as you navigate it, if that's the case for you. If you have never contributed post-tax money to your Traditional IRA, then you don't have to worry about the pro-rata rule.

Asset location and capital gains

You may have heard of asset allocation from the investing chapters, but have you heard of asset location? This is not about what assets you have in a portfolio, but more about what types of ACCOUNTS you hold your assets in for capital gains tax purposes.

This is in relation to paper assets like stocks or bonds; but if you hold an asset for under one year, your income is taxed as ordinary income and moves through the tax brackets that I outlined a few sections ago. But guess what? If you hold your assets for OVER one year, you are eligible for a more favorable tax rate! It's called long-term capital gains tax, and the difference in taxation can be fairly large.

The wealthy take advantage of long-term capital gains rates.

This is where asset location comes in. It could make more sense for something like expected highly appreciating stock to be held in a taxable brokerage account instead of a tax-deferred traditional retirement account. This is due to long-term capital gains rates being much lower at the time of this writing than having it in a Traditional IRA where you will have to pay regular income taxes on it later (assuming tax rates stay the same for your retirement years).

Keep in mind, the capital gains tax brackets that would apply to you are based on your taxable income (including your capital gains). They are also progressive as well, so you could end up with capital gains moving through multiple brackets depending on your income and how large your capital gain is.

Here are the capital gains tax brackets for 2024 (always check for updates yearly as the IRS adjusts income for inflation):

2024 long-term capital gains tax rates and brackets

Tax-filing status	0% tax rate	15% tax rate	20% tax rate
Single	$0 to $47,025.	$47,026 to $518,900.	$518,901 or more.
Married, filing jointly	$0 to $94,050.	$94,051 to $583,750.	$583,751 or more.
Married, filing separately	$0 to $47,025.	$47,026 to $291,850.	$291,851 or more.
Head of household	$0 to $63,000.	$63,001 to $551,350.	$551,351 or more.

Source: NerdWallet.com

Controlling income

Being aware of your income can help you know when to pull certain levers to control taxation. Some common strategies here could be selectively timing when you sell stock or other assets, taking on less work to keep your income under a certain amount to qualify for tax credits, or taking on more medical bills and charitable giving in a single year to take advantage of a large itemized deduction in a given year.

Tax-Free Money That You Maybe Don't Know Exists!

Believe it or not, there are some pretty amazing ways to avoid taxation on some money completely! These are probably the best kept secrets of our tax code right here:

1. **Section 121 Exclusion (aka exclusion of capital gains in your home)**

This is a very handy piece of the tax code that helps homeowners. If you sell your primary residence and make more than what you paid for the home, you may qualify for up to $250,000 if you're single ($500,000 if married filing jointly) free of capital gains tax completely. Yes, you read that right: no tax!

You have to meet two tests: You have 1) owned **and** 2) used your home as your main home for a period aggregating at least two years out of the five years prior to its date of sale, according to IRS.gov.

This isn't necessarily a reason to go out and sell your home if you want to stay there, but when you do decide to sell, it's a nice benefit.

2. **Roth IRAs**

We've talked about Roth IRAs a lot throughout this book, but it's worth another mention here because even though you pay tax on contributions going in, the gains you make in your account come out tax-free in retirement via qualified distributions. If you have a lot of time to let investments work, boy, is this a powerful account!

High income earners typically don't qualify for contributing to a Roth IRA, and the more income you earn (and higher tax rates you pay), the more analysis needs to go into this decision. However, for the majority of people in America, a Roth is a great tool to build some tax-free wealth.

To give you an idea, as of this writing, a couple with modified adjusted gross income at or above $206,000 can't contribute to a Roth at all. They could, however, convert Traditional IRA funds into a Roth IRA if they choose.

3. **Health Savings Accounts (HSA)**

We call this the triple-threat of tax savings in the finance world, because it's such a powerful account. As of this writing, you have to have a high-deductible healthcare plan that meets certain criteria in order to be eligible to contribute to an HSA. However, if you can, it should be one of the first places you allocate money to.

Why?

First of all, the contributions to these accounts are tax-deductible up to the contribution limit.

Second, this money can actually be invested and grow over time potentially tax-free.

Third, if you spend the money (and its growth) on qualified healthcare expenses, you're paying with money that hasn't been taxed at all. That's powerful!

And getting old is expensive, so if you don't use the money right away, you can use it later in your golden years (even for Part B Medicare premiums that you'll have to pay later. Nope, Medicare isn't free!).

What's even cooler? If you don't need the account for medical expenses ever in your life, or don't have enough medical expenses to use it up, you can simply withdraw the money in a similar fashion to a Traditional IRA for anything non-medical at the age of 65. You'll just pay taxes on the withdrawals for anything not medical related.

Yep, it just turns into a regular Traditional IRA if you want it to! So there isn't much to lose here with an HSA.

4. **Qualified small business stock**

Investing in small businesses has its perks. If you have a gain from qualifying small business stock, you can completely avoid taxation up to certain generous limits for stock acquired after September 27, 2010. Yes, 100% of your gain could be completely tax-free.

My husband and I had invested in a startup years back, and we were actually able to take advantage of this exclusion ourselves. It's amazing.

If you think this could apply to you, I suggest consulting with a Certified Public Accountant (CPA), as there are some tests that the stock has to pass to qualify.

Taxes Directly Affect Your Wealth

I know taxes are intimidating and confusing.

This is why financial professionals make the big bucks, because most people don't even know anything that is in these past few chapters. But this has been a big issue I have had with our education system for years.

Taxation affects almost everyone throughout all parts of life (working, having kids, investing, selling a home, and even death).

I notice most people are waiting until the last minute and scrambling, likely overpaying on taxes because they are just unaware of how the system works and how to prepare and strategize year round. Or they have a tax professional, but just do what they say without having any idea what it all means (been there, done that).

So you are actually ahead of most by just getting some new vocabulary under your belt. You'll also be able to work with your tax professional more efficiently, which I think is important.

As I mentioned before, re-read this chapter. Repetition is key with this type of quantitative (and heavy) information.

Taxation has a DIRECT effect on how much wealth you can build. If you can learn and strategize better, you will go far with your money.

JOURNAL:

What is your adjusted gross income (AGI)?
(In 2021, it was line 11 on the 1040.)

Part VI

Design Your Legacy

Chapter 11
Securing Your Family's Future

We've covered a lot so far around the why and how of working toward your definition of financial freedom.

As we come out of the tax chapters, I just want to commend you on making it this far!

I know many of these topics can be heavy, but if I did my job right, you're going to be better prepared to manage your money with a bit more confidence.

The Only Things Certain in Life Are Death and Taxes

If we think about everything that we do to get to this point, making sure our cash goes to the right places, putting the right insurance in place, choosing retirement accounts, and getting invested, we've put in a lot of effort to make sure our financial life is in order.

Something not always at the forefront of our minds while doing all of this? Death.

We plan for this inevitable event with estate planning, but it's commonly not something people tend to think about until way down the road ... sometimes too far down the road.

So, the point of this chapter and the next is to help you learn why and how to prepare so that everything you worked your tail off to earn passes the way you want it to ... and more!

This isn't just about your assets passing to the right place. It's also about who will take care of your dependents, how your bills will get paid so that you don't leave your loved ones with a big burden, how someone can get access to your health information if you are in the hospital, and more.

So, if you think you don't have enough assets for estate planning ... think again! It goes way beyond just your assets.

It's Normal to Feel Weird About This

Let me make this clear ... if you're feeling strange or uncomfortable about thinking about the end of your life, you're not alone! It's totally normal.

I am a financial planner, and even I had some unexpected uneasy feelings when I was sitting down with my estate attorney. So go into this prepared for the funny feelings.

However, that aside, this is an essential part of sound finances, and you will sleep better at night knowing that if something happens to you, your loved ones will be okay.

Allow yourself to start this process with recognizing who you want to:

1. Take care of your minor children if something happens to you.
2. Take care of your financial affairs if you become incapacitated.
3. Take care of your health affairs and get health information.

4. Receive your assets if you pass.
5. Be the executor of your estate (this person handles a lot of the logistics of making sure everything gets done right).

So it takes some consideration and discussions with people who may fill some of these duties for you.

Consider, for example, having a talk with your mom/dad/aunt/uncle/best friend about taking care of your minor children if something happens to you. You want to make sure that whoever takes on the responsibility is willing and able. This is for your peace of mind and for everyone else involved.

If this planning doesn't get done, the state will take the liberty of choosing something like who will take care of your children for you. Many people do not like the idea of this!

Incapacity and Health Planning

You probably caught by now that estate planning goes way past just planning for who gets your money and assets. So if you don't have a lot of assets, that doesn't mean you shouldn't have an estate plan.

A very important part of estate planning is preparing for what would happen if you became incapacitated for any amount of time. Simply put, this means if you become mentally or physically unable to perform your daily essential activities like pay your bills or make important life decisions.

I hope this never happens to you, but if it does and you don't have a plan in place, the courts appoint someone to take care of your affairs. Dealing with the courts is not a fun or necessarily cheap process. Remember, this person who gets appointed will have full control over your finances or your life! So you want someone you trust.

A proper estate plan will ensure you have a financial power of attorney in place. This power of attorney will become active upon you becoming incapacitated.

Another important part of estate planning would be healthcare planning.

In this case, you'll want to assign someone a healthcare power of attorney that will become active if you become incapacitated. This will ensure someone can legally make healthcare decisions on your behalf. You'll also want to have a HIPAA (Health Insurance Portability and Accountability Act) authorization drafted, which will outline who is allowed to get access to your healthcare status and information.

Again, the idea is that nothing terrible ever happens to you and you won't have to use these important documents. However, it's just like obtaining insurance. You hope you won't have to use it, but you're glad you have it if you do ever need it.

Probate

We can't talk about estate planning without discussing probate first. Understanding probate is the key to getting you to make moves quicker than you would have otherwise.

Probate is a court process in which a judge will interpret your Last Will and Testament documents and pass your assets based on what this document says.

This is where a well written will is important. You want your wishes to be clearly expressed. Any confusion could lead the court to make some decisions.

When a family member has to go through the probate process, the Last Will and Testament documents are actually publicly filed with the court. This makes your loved one's will public record.

If you value privacy, probate may not be something you want your family to go through.

There are two main ways that you can completely avoid probate, and I will cover them in the next chapter in detail for you.

Do You Need an Attorney?

Many people ask me, "Can I just make a will on a site like LegalZoom.com or something similar?"

The short answer is, if you can't afford an attorney, or you just need to have something on record quickly until you can get a will done professionally, you can use a site like this to create a will.

If you have a very simple situation, you may have no issues. However, I do strongly recommend working with an attorney in your state to create a will for you.

An attorney can be sure that a will is written for your specific needs and within the state laws.

Long-Term Care Insurance

Long-term care is health care that helps you with essential daily activities if you can't perform them yourself due to illness.

Think of activities like showering, toileting, general hygiene, walking, transferring from a bed to a chair, eating, or dressing. If you can't do a few of these things, you may need long-term care.

This probably belongs more in the insurance chapter; however, I am going to bring this topic of long-term care insurance into the estate planning chapter for a few reasons.

First of all, long-term care is typically utilized closer to the end of your life.

Long-term care is extraordinarily expensive, and Medicare doesn't even cover long-term care if it's the only care you need (Medicare may cover long-term care up to a certain number of days if you also need medical care with it).

Financial planners have moved away from suggesting long-term care insurance due to the high costs. Instead, many have suggested "self-insuring" by planning early in life and investing the money you'd pay on an insurance policy.

It's very difficult to say what end-of-life care will look like for everyone, so it's important to consider your health, your age, who you have in your life to help take care of you, and how much a long-term care policy will actually cost.

Then, you can estimate if it makes more sense to own a policy or save and invest the money yourself.

Keep in mind that after a certain age, and if you're in bad health, it may be very difficult and expensive to even obtain a long-term care policy. Early planning is important here!

Stay Calm and Estate Plan

If you're still feeling the heebie-jeebies about planning for how your assets will pass on to the next generation, I encourage you to reframe your thinking.

Instead of fear around it, envision the way your assets can help people who you love.

Imagine your favorite people (whether it's family or friends) having a more enriched life.

Imagine your favorite charities inheriting assets that will help them make change in communities.

This is your legacy!

Journal:

Do you have a will? Has it been updated recently? If not, write down some attorneys to call and get a cost quote here:

Who in your life would you like to pass assets to?

Who in your life would you like to be responsible for your children? Who do you trust to handle your financial affairs? What about your healthcare affairs?

Write them all down. They can all be separate people for different responsibilities.

Chapter 12
Avoid the Biggest Estate Planning Mistakes

In the previous chapter, we covered why estate planning is for everyone (not just the wealthy).

We also covered why a living will and testament alone will not necessarily help you avoid probate.

In this chapter, we will dive into ways to avoid probate in more detail, how passing assets can help your loved ones save on taxes, and some tips for those who are more philanthropic.

Horror Estate Stories

I have story after story of estate planning gone wrong (or not at all). You may have actually gone through some estate planning horror stories yourself.

The first thing to mention is that all families have unique situations. Maybe you have a blended family. It's possible you may have a disabled child or spouse. You may even have a family feud going on and you don't want certain family members to get your assets or custody of your children.

I think back to a family of five children. They all inherited a home from their father. One child, who happened to be the black sheep, was basically living in the house they had all inherited, against the will of the other four siblings.

The sibling living in the inherited house technically owns part of the home. He has the legal right to be in the home. However, he doesn't contribute to the bills or allow the rest of the siblings to renovate and rent out the house.

The attorney basically told them there isn't much legally they can do about it unless they sell the house. The idea of selling the house is gut-wrenching to the siblings, as it was a spot where family reunions were held and memories were made. The parent who is deceased didn't take the conflicts into account when passing down the home.

Now it's left to the siblings to deal with the problem, and they possibly have to make a very hard decision of selling the house if they can't all agree.

How could that have been solved? Perhaps splitting the home among the children who wanted it and providing a cash inheritance for the children who didn't or couldn't keep up with the expenses of maintaining it.

Another story that I hear of is inheritances going to heirs with disabilities. Why is this a problem, you ask? Well, people with disabilities are often on government programs. If they inherit too many assets, they may not qualify for their government assistance. This is a big problem for those in need.

Proper estate planning can solve this problem by making sure a special needs trust is created and assets pass into the trust, not to the individual with the disability.

Another big problem that I see often is heirs inheriting money who are not very responsible with money in the first place. If you have a lot of money and a fiscally irresponsible

around and find someone who you think would be good to work with.

The good news about the fee for getting a living will created is this typically comes with extra essentials that you'll need. For example, a "pourover will" to catch any assets you don't put into the trust, medical power of attorney, durable power of attorney, incapacity document, and HIPAA authorization document.

One last thought: a revocable living trust lets you keep 100% control over your assets, so this type of trust doesn't provide asset protection for you from creditors. However, it will provide protection from creditors to your heirs when they inherit the assets. Talk to your attorney about this if it's a concern!

Giving to Charities

Some people are very philanthropically inclined. If that's you, there are great ways to give to charity.

You can set charities as beneficiaries on your accounts. You may also set up certain types of charitable trusts that allow you to take advantage of your assets while you're alive.

Charitable Remainder Unitrusts (CRUTs) are trusts created that allow you to transfer assets to the trust in return for

1. A charitable tax deduction for part of the transfer.
2. An income stream to an income beneficiary (this can be you or someone else).
3. A donation of the remainder of the assets to the designated charity upon your death.

I suggest talking to an estate attorney to implement any trust strategies!

Step Up in Basis—The Tax-Saving Estate Planning Tool You Didn't Know About

One big secret to most people is taking advantage of the "step up in basis" tax rule.

Wealthy people know about it, because they have advisors helping them. So I'm going to tell you this secret so that you can strategize like the wealthy.

When assets are given to you during the giftor's life, you inherit their "cost basis" in that asset. Said more simply, if your dad gives you a house or some Apple stock, for example, when they give it to you, what they paid is going to be what you paid for tax purposes.

So going with my example, if your dad gave you a house, and he paid $100,000 for it, when you go to sell it later, and if it has appreciated to $300,000, you'll owe taxes on the profits. You inherited his cost basis. You would owe capital gains taxes on $200,000 (the $300,000 it's worth, minus the $100,000 your dad paid for it).

Now, say instead of your dad giving it to you during his life, you inherited the house upon his death.

This is the power of the step up in basis rule. The cost basis you will have in the home becomes the value of the house upon your dad's passing. So when you sell it, the cost basis "steps up." It's a beautiful thing.

So, let's assume now that you inherit the house upon your dad's passing instead. Upon his passing, the house was worth

$300,000. You decide you don't want to keep the house, and you sell it right away. You will owe NO—yes, I said NO—capital gains taxes in this case.

You went from having taxes owed on a $200,000 capital gain by the home being gifted during your dad's life to a ZERO tax bill by inheriting upon his death.

I'll take it a step further to really drive home the logistics. Say your dad passes and you inherit the home. The home is valued at that same $300,000. But you don't want to sell it. You want to keep it for a few more years. When the years pass and you're ready to sell, it's worth $350,000. This will leave you owing taxes on a $50,000 capital gain (the $350,000 it's worth today, minus the $300,000 value the house was when your dad passed).

So, I hope these three examples drive the point home of how this can be a powerful way to pass down assets ... ESPECIALLY highly appreciated ones!

I'm So Proud

So now I hope you have a better understanding of why estate planning is for everyone and why it's so important.

I am confident that I have given you not only some strategies you can implement right away but also ways to think about saving taxes, making sure your children are well taken care of, and more.

If you've made it this far in this book, you are truly in the minority of people, those who are actively working to better their finances.

I am extremely proud of you!

JOURNAL:

What accounts or life insurance policies can you set beneficiaries on or update your existing beneficiaries on?

Conclusion

Congratulations! You've done something that most people will not do. You have taken time out of your busy life to commit to learning how to manage your money better.

Money is not the be-all and end-all to happiness, but it does make life a lot easier once you achieve your version of financial freedom (remember, it's not a one-size-fits-all definition).

You're now one step closer to:

- Avoiding expensive financial mistakes
- Understanding how to set lifestyle and financial goals
- Knowing what types of accounts to invest in
- Protecting your loved ones in case something happens to you
- Strategizing taxes more efficiently, and more

Remember, your definition of financial freedom is achieved through optimizing the six major puzzle pieces:

1. Cash flow management

2. Risk protection
3. Retirement planning
4. Investment optimization
5. Tax strategy
6. Planning your legacy

You need all of these puzzle pieces working together holistically!

Still confused?

You may still be feeling a little lost or overwhelmed with all of this information in the book.

I want you to know that this is normal!

The point of this book was for you to gain a baseline of knowledge to take things to the next level. Everyone has to start somewhere, and this book was that start to get your wheels turning.

I have a few suggestions if you're still feeling lost or overwhelmed.

For one, re-read each chapter, one at a time, then implement one action for that specific puzzle piece being discussed. Don't move on until you've fully understood a term I used or an action you should be doing. Use the internet to do extra research to make sure you feel comfortable before moving on.

Don't forget, there are journal exercises at the end of each chapter to get you thinking about important parts of your money life that you may not have thought about before.

Secondly, sometimes video helps more than reading a book. I simply can't convey the message as easily in words on paper as I can in video with live examples. This is why my masterclasses are pretty popular.

I suggest going to https://shetalksfinance.com to find my offerings that will help you get more visual and detailed education.

I have video content that is free on my YouTube channel and a premium training program as well. You can find all of my offerings directly on my website.

I am here to help you take the next steps with your money. So let's connect on social media as well! I am at @shetalksfinance across all major social media channels. As a matter of fact, do me a favor by posting and tagging me in a picture of this book if you found it helpful!

I do believe that a more financially educated world is a better world. Thank you for being a part of making your own life and the world a better place and more financially independent!

About the Author

Nikki Dunn is a CERTIFIED FINANCIAL PLANNER™ professional with a passion for helping professionals and business owners understand and manage their money better. She has been trading and investing in the stock market for over a decade and has run multiple seven-figure online businesses. She started She Talks Finance, an education platform to help more do-it-yourself investor types to get access to sound financial information. She has taught thousands of people how to not only master their personal finances, but also build better investment portfolios, manage their money mindset, and master tax strategies. She has been featured as an expert in articles on Bloomberg, Yahoo Finance, Next Advisor, Financial Advisor, and more.

Made in United States
Orlando, FL
04 November 2026

90221056R00115